Eagles

has lived by herself now for a g⸺ ⸺⸺⸺.
From a long way off we saw her, like a white spot
on the cliff, below the old nest, which is still
there, on a high cliff, over the sea, about 500 ft.
in height. She was very mild, and flew off
and away, while we were yet a long way off
and we did not see her again. She is quite
white, looks as white as a gull while flying.
We went into a natural shelter about 150 yds. off.
this shelter was a big crack, or chimney, with a
split in the side opposite to the entrance. from
where we could look across to the nest, which was
about 100 ft. from the top of the cliff. I spent a
time here making an oil sketch of the nesting
cliff. But it was a horrid cramped position,
and a bad afternoon, blowing half a gale of wind
and driving thick # drizzling mist across.
But I was fairly well sheltered and worked
for 1½ hours, and then was too cramped and
cold to continue, so went home in the rain.
June. 30. Very windy. Went again to see the
Eagle. She was not in sight when we got
there. It was too windy to paint, so I made a
pencil sketch of the rock in the immediate vicinity
of the nest.     While so engaged, a hoodie crow
continually mobbed something round the corner,

# MEMOIRS OF AN ARTIST NATURALIST

## NEW EDITION BY GEORGE EDWARD LODGE TRUST

This George Edward Lodge Trust edition edited by
Brian Bird, Chairman of the George Edward Lodge Trust.

First published in Great Britain in 1946 by Gurney and Jackson.

This edition published by the George Edward Lodge Trust in 2013.

© George Edward Lodge Trust 2013

British Library Cataloguing in Publication Data.

A CIP record for this book is available from the British Library.

ISBN 978-0-9562946-1-6

Printed and bound in Great Britain by Butler Tanner & Dennis Ltd, Frome, Somerset, BA11 1NF, UK.

Front and back endpapers are reproductions of pages from George Lodge's *Memoirs* manuscript.

George Edward Lodge
1860 – 1954

Pencil drawing by Judith Magill.

*What a lesson to all of us, what a life to have led. To have made a living out of the thing you liked best in the world. To have known that your work sends those who see it back delightedly in thought to the salmon river, the forest, the crags and the hills, and the deer and the birds they have watched there.*

From J.K. Stanford's obituary of
George Lodge in *The Field*, 25th February 1954.

# MEMOIRS OF AN ARTIST NATURALIST

## NEW EDITION BY GEORGE EDWARD LODGE TRUST

The George Edward Lodge Trust has decided to republish this edition of *Memoirs of an Artist Naturalist*, for several reasons. Firstly to advance education of the public in the artwork, life and skills of George E. Lodge - this aim is paramount to the charity. Secondly, the first edition of *Memoirs* was published in 1946, sadly lacking in those days the printing quality it so rightly deserved. Paper and metal printing plates were not at their best just after the Second World War.

George Lodge was far too modest to have photographs of himself put in *Memoirs*, and mentioned very little about his early life. So, on reflection it was decided by the Trustees that a more definitive biography was required for the record. Fortunately for the Trust, Judith Magill, Trustee and George Lodge's great niece has risen to the challenge to write this touching biography. Also, a variety of artwork was selected for the gallery section to show Lodge's immense talent as the complete artist.

I was extremely privileged to have known the late R.B. (Dick) Treleaven, MBE, who was a Trustee and George Lodge's last pupil. His stories of the frequent meetings with Lodge at Hawkhouse were always captivating. Dick never forgot Lodge's tremendous enthusiasm and sense of humour, which never diminished despite his age. On one occasion, Lodge said, "We painters should be allowed to live to be at least a thousand years, then perhaps we could get an inkling of our trade."

George Lodge wrote and illustrated his only book *Memoirs of an Artist Naturalist*, at the age of eighty-five. The wealth of material within these pages resulted from a lifetime of "finding out". His writings on acute observations and his artistic genius will enrich and enhance the wildlife artist, naturalist, ornithologist, falconer and all devotees of natural history.

Brian Bird
George Edward Lodge Trust Chairman

Iceland gyr-falcon.  From George Lodge's field sketch book, 1880s or 90s.
Pen and ink drawing.

Bramblings. From George Lodge's field sketch book, 1880s or 90s.
Watercolour.

## ACKNOWLEDGEMENTS

There are many people whose help has been invaluable in preparing this new publication of *Memoirs of an Artist Naturalist*. Some have allowed pictures to be photographed, others have been available with advice and reminiscences of George Lodge, and some have supplied photographs and transparencies.

They include: The late Brenda Lodge, the late Harry Savory, the late R.B. (Dick) Treleaven, MBE, Karen Bird, Stewart Canham, Douglas Mann, Michael Mann, Bridget Miller Mundy, Tony Nash, MBE, John Southern, OBE, Gordon Templeton, Tryon Gallery, and Michael and June Woodford.

Special thanks are due to all the Lodge descendants in Australia for their contributions.

G.E.L. Trust

Opposite: Sea eagle mobbed by hooded crows - one of the two dust jackets from the original 1946 edition. The other - Kite, with nest - can be seen in *Memoirs*.

# MEMOIRS
## OF AN
# ARTIST NATURALIST

## GEORGE E. LODGE
### F.Z.S., F.R.E.S., VICE-PRES. B.O.U

*24 PLATES ...of which... 16 IN COLOUR*

BLACK JES

# MEMOIRS OF AN ARTIST NATURALIST

BY

## GEORGE E. LODGE

F.Z.S., F.R.E.S., VICE-PRES. BRIT. ORN. UNION

ILLUSTRATED WITH 24 PLATES
OF WHICH 16 ARE IN COLOUR

GURNEY AND JACKSON
LONDON: 98 GREAT RUSSELL STREET, W.C.
EDINBURGH: TWEEDDALE COURT
1946

*frontispiece*

BLACK JESS
Intermewed eyass falcon. Trained and flown by the late Kim Muir,
10th Royal Hussars.

PRINTED IN GREAT BRITAIN BY
OLIVER AND BOYD LTD., EDINBURGH

# CONTENTS

## PART I

### HAWKS AND HAWKING

## PART II

### WOODLAND AND MARSH

## PART III

### SOME SHETLAND MEMORIES

## PART IV

### MEMORIES OF GAME BIRDS

## PART V

# ILLUSTRATIONS

## COLOUR PLATES

## BLACK AND WHITE PLATES

PEREGRINE, WITH EYASSES

On the "Seven Sisters." Sussex Coast. June 15, 1933.

# PART I

## HAWKS AND HAWKING

### I. The Peregrine Falcon

THE peregrine falcon (*Falco peregrinus peregrinus* Tunst.) is much commoner in this country than is generally supposed. It occurs frequently in autumn and winter in parts where it is rarely seen at other times, because northern-bred birds are then making their way south. These migrants often stay several weeks in a district where food, such as partridges and woodpigeons, is plentiful. The sea-cliffs of the British Isles provide many breeding sites, and so do the mountainous parts of Scotland and Wales.

Preservation of game has no doubt lessened the numbers of the peregrine, but other factors such as the shrinking of areas on which desirable prey is present must also have played their part. There is little fear, anyway, that game preservation will cause the falcon to be exterminated, for it is well able to take care of itself, and the wilder parts of the country provide good sanctuary. I have many notes of having seen wild peregrines during days of shooting and hawking in Norfolk and Lincolnshire, where I have spent much of my time.

There seems to be a strong prejudice in some places against flying trained hawks over preserved ground, the argument being that the presence of the hawk tends to drive away permanently the existing stock of game, *i.e.* grouse and partridges. I think this idea is based more on fancy than fact. I have seen the same ground used for game hawking with peregrines for weeks at a time, flying the hawks at least three times each week and sometimes more, without any noticeable falling-off in the quantity of game.

When one comes to examine the facts, there seems little reason why game should leave. The peregrine is the natural enemy of game birds and they must often see wild peregrines—especially on the Scottish grouse moors. It does not frighten them unduly as long as they sit close until the hawk is out of sight. No one has ever heard of the presence of a wild falcon *denuding* a moor or a manor of game. It takes a variable toll, but the coveys will not leave the ground for such a reason. Their strong sense of home ground would not allow them to be so easily disturbed.

A

After all, the upset from hawking is nothing like so great as when the birds are being driven over guns.

In hawking, all the birds over a wide expanse of country will see the falcon " waiting on " at a very high pitch, but only the individual covey put up for her will be disturbed. Of course, it must be admitted that the ground is left *entirely* undisturbed for much longer periods when shot over than when hawked.

Peregrines flying over have the effect of making game birds lie close. Eagles have just the opposite effect. In Scotland it is well known how the appearance of an eagle over the skyline will clear a whole glen of grouse—to the great discomfiture of driving operations that may be in progress. The grouse will come back again soon, it is true, but many a day's shooting has been spoilt, or partly spoilt, by the presence of an eagle.

The peregrine takes its prey on the wing, and the game birds seem to have developed to a high degree the power of distinguishing between the ground-hunting eagle and buzzard, and the falcon. In her presence they exhibit the different reaction of lying close. Duck, curlew, gulls—all are prey for the peregrine ; her powers of sight are very great and she may make a flight of miles to knock a bird more or less dead to the ground or, " trussing " it, carry it to some convenient place to eat at her leisure.

Where a peregrine inhabits a sea-cliff near colonies of puffins, flights are made along the cliff face and a puffin flying forth or coming home is sure to fall victim. These birds are often taken to a dub of water and thoroughly wetted before the peregrine plucks them. The reaction of lying close in the presence of the falcon is nothing like so highly developed in cliff-breeding birds as in game, though black guillemots or tysties when attacked over the sea will fall like stones to the water and disappear below the surface.

The falcon receives a good deal of inadvertent help in getting grouse flushed for her by the passage of a shepherd or his dogs over the ground, a stalker or a gillie with a pony, or even innocent people searching for white heather. A peregrine does not wait for weak or sickly birds to get up, but goes for the first seen on a covey rising. I have many times seen trained peregrines kill the leading bird of a covey of grouse or partridges, and if a trained bird will do this it seems reasonable to suppose a wild bird would do the same. Healthy birds are much the more likely to be first on the wing than the sickly ones.

The so-called balance of nature, which in truth is not so much a balance as a see-sawing, pendulum-like movement, is inevitably much upset in civilised countries, for certain predatory animals have to be kept in check in order to maintain flocks and herds and even the amenities of settled life. We " farm " our game birds and animals to some extent, and to ensure a more or less steady crop some of the predatory species have at least to be lessened. There has been a steady advance towards an enlightened policy of game preservation, and we may hope the future will see all keepers, lessees and proprietors conserving game with greater knowledge of the true role of some animals and birds which formerly shamed the vermin pole. Long may the peregrine falcon persist in a world of live and let live !

## Game Hawking

It is the invariable habit of the peregrine to strike its prey with the feet, which are so well furnished with claws that can grip and take up the shock of impact. If a peregrine, coming down from a height at the tremendous pace which it does when stooping, were to hit its quarry with its breast bone—as is alleged by some people—it would bruise itself to such an extent that, if not killed on the spot, it would certainly succumb eventually from inflammation of the crop.

I have seen scores of grouse, partridges and rooks killed by trained peregrines ; and when exercising hawks to the swung lure it is quite easy to see what happens from a distance of a very few yards. Immediately before striking, the feet are thrust forward and the lure either struck or seized by the claws ; and then, of course, there is sufficient play for the backward swing of the legs as the hawk rakes headlong forward over the object struck. Even so, the shock is often sufficient to kill the quarry. If the hawk were to keep the feet rigid when striking, the inevitable result would be broken legs. The terrific force with which a resolute hawk comes down on to a grouse must be seen to be believed. The grouse is knocked head over heels amid a cloud of flying feathers and the bird bounces up again when it hits the ground ; and yet I have often seen the quarry immediately start running to dodge the hawk, which is now trying to take it from the ground. If the hawk settles, as it often will in its effort to catch the quarry, the grouse may take to wing again, clean outfly the hawk and escape. A grouse with its short, rapidly-moving wings can leave the ground much quicker than a long-winged hawk and can therefore get well under way with a good chance of escaping.

A few years ago Captain G. Blaine had a very active and clever tiercel which was remarkably good at catching an active grouse on the ground after it had been knocked down in the stoop. Few birds would escape him under these circumstances. He was also a very high flier and would wait on very steadily once he got his pitch. His name was Hector. I have seen him hunting his grouse which he had knocked down into heather, bracken or turnips. Every time the grouse tried to get up and fly, Hector was off the ground at once and so quickly that the grouse had nothing else to do but put in again, and the tiercel was almost always taken up with the grouse in his foot.

A tiercel, of course, is much quicker off the spot and more active in turning than a falcon; and this in some measure compensates for his lack of weight, which is so necessary to enable a hawk to give a knock-out blow to such a strong quarry as a grouse. The average weight of a cock grouse is greater than that of a peregrine tiercel.

On the whole, falcons are more suitable for grouse and tiercels for partridges. I have seen many wild peregrines, though I have never yet seen one actually strike its quarry, so I have been unable to compare the style of a wild hawk with the many trained ones I have known and seen fly.

The late Major Fisher, in his book *Reminiscences of a Falconer*, maintains that the worst wild hawk is of necessity better than the best trained one. I cannot agree with this, for I have seen such excellent trained hawks that it is not easy to imagine a wild hawk being better than they were. Doubtless a wild hawk has much more flying exercise than falls to the lot of trained hawks and would therefore be stronger on the wing for longer times. With so much more practice it would be a better " footer." Passage hawks are for this reason to be preferred to eyasses for rook hawking, the rook being a very active and elusive quarry. But I think there may be trained hawks which might beat wild ones in style and also in pace.

I once saw a wild falcon join a trained one which was flying a grouse and it appeared to me slower than the trained bird. Of course, one could not tell whether she was trying her best or not and she may have had half a crop in her at the time. This incident occurred when hawking with Gilbert Blaine in Caithness. Here is the note from my diary :

" *September* 22, 1913. The hawks killed 13 grouse to-day. During one flight when Sylvia was up, a wild falcon came and joined in. Sylvia was flying a covey which went over a cottage on a small holding, the wild hawk following hard after. One of the grouse put in to some cabbages and this we got as we ran after. By this time they were all out of sight so we ran on in the direction they had gone ; and before long found the wild hawk sitting on a fence post. She went off again pretty wild, and we scouted around feeling sure that Sylvia must be on her quarry in the vicinity; and we soon found her among the grasses and rushes, pluming her grouse."

This hawk, Sylvia, was a young eyass falcon, and her score for that season was 90 grouse and 3 sundries out of 96 flights. Could any wild falcon do better at such strong, heavy quarry? Another young eyass falcon, Nora, that same season killed 81 grouse and one sundry out of 90 flights.

First-rate dogs are essential for grouse hawking. With partridges they are not so necessary, as one can flush a covey and generally mark them down. You then know when to put up your hawk. But grouse take much longer flights, seldom alighting again in sight, and you must know where they are before hooding off the hawk; and this can be done best with the aid of a dog.

When grouse are found, the hawk cast off and she has obtained her pitch, the grouse must be flushed downwind in order to give the hawk the best chance in her stoop. Wary eyes must be kept on the hawk all the time during this operation so as to avoid flushing the grouse during the time she may be raking a bit wide or, in the course of her circling, happens to have her tail instead of her head towards the scene of action. If she is waiting-on very high and well overhead when the grouse are flushed, she will immediately give one or two very rapid flicks with her wings and then, closing them at the tips, come rushing down in a stupendous vertical stoop, the air singing audibly through her feathers and bells, and in a cloud of feathers a fairly hit grouse will be knocked headlong to the ground, perhaps before he has had time to fly farther than thirty or forty yards.

A peregrine may often be placed at such an angle to the direction of the flushed quarry that her stoop may be begun more or less across the line of flight, and it is then beautiful to see a hawk that knows her work twist like lightning in her stoop to get her direction in the same line as that which her quarry is taking. Failing to do this will almost certainly result in a miss. I have many times seen young hawks attempt stooping across the line of flight, but have only once seen it successful. A good hawk very soon learns the futility of such tactics.

One of the most unusual kills I ever saw was with Blaine and his hawks in Islay. Again referring to my diary:

"*September* 17, 1938. . . . we had a very long tramp before getting another point. Cressida was put up to this. She did not get to any height but was well placed when a small covey got up. She stooped at one which went to the left and which put in almost immediately into the bracken. Cressida left this grouse and made a right-angled crash at the rest of the covey, which were about forty yards off to the right, and knocked a grouse stone dead. It fell straight to the ground and she went down at once to it."

This was certainly extraordinary, for when the hawk left the first grouse she was on the same level as the rest of the covey out of which she made her kill. I once saw, also, a peregrine cut the head clean off her quarry when she struck; but it was so long ago I cannot remember whether it was a falcon with a grouse or a tiercel with a partridge.

## Rook Hawking

Rook hawking is beautiful sport of quite different quality to that of game hawking. Instead of the high, steady waiting-on before the quarry is flushed and then the magnificent stooping from a height at a fast-flying quarry only a few feet from the ground, the hawk is flown from the hand direct at the rooks after having made an upwind approach as near as possible to the quarry —which may be several hundred yards—and then a fine exhibition of tactics takes place. The quarry does its best to get above the hawk in the sky and the hawk forces the quarry upwind, at the same time ringing to get above; which aim being effected, the rook is forced to drop downwind and then the hawk puts in her stoop.

A rook is surprisingly active when being hunted by a peregrine and will sideslip time after time, just at the psychological moment, so foiling stoop after stoop, and often escaping altogether. The stoops under these circumstances are generally short ones and take place in rapid succession; but after each stoop missed the hawk has lost ground—or rather air—and must get above her quarry again. A quick throw up will attain this before the rook has made much to his advantage. All this invariably takes place in a downwind direction, and at last the rook, finding himself unequal to keeping himself safely above his assailant, makes a long downward slide towards any kind of cover that may be available—trees, sheepfolds, hedges, even an isolated gorse bush— in hopes of escaping. This is the hawk's last chance; but if she misses her stoop the quarry will almost always escape, unless someone of the field can get up in time to help the hawk, by ejecting the rook every time it puts in from the hawk's attacks. A rook is far more active on the ground and dodging round fences, or in a tree, than a peregrine. Once a rook takes refuge in a clump of trees he is quite safe, as nothing will induce him to leave such a sanctuary. I have once seen a rook taken by hand on a fence after having put in under a hawk, rather than face the hawk again in the open.

I have only once seen a hawk capable of catching a rook in a tree ; this was an eyass tiercel called Rufus, flown on Salisbury Plain by R. Spens in 1937. There was a certain tree by a small farmhouse, which was a favourite refuge for rooks that were being flown in the neighbourhood. On one occasion a rook was being flown by Rufus and put into some stacks as the hawk stooped at it. The tiercel tried to catch the rook on the ground there, but of course the rook dodged round the stack and got away out of sight of the hawk. Spens had run up just in time to help his hawk, of which he seized hold and flung after the rook, now a hundred yards away. The hawk chased the rook to this tree by the farm, hunted it through the branches of the tree, forced it to the ground and took it there. The next day the same hawk was slipped at a rook on passage in the same neighbourhood. The rook after being well flown took refuge in the same tree, where a carrion crow joined in to mob the hawk. But the crow had made a bad mistake, for he was caught in the tree by the tiercel.

I think that crows are more easily caught by peregrines than are rooks, as crows are not so active at dodging a peregrine's stoop but they are apt to be more dangerous to the hawk. In the spring rook-hawking time the crows are paired and the mate of one that has been caught by a hawk, if anywhere in sight or hearing, will come and savagely attack the hawk. The least that may happen is that the hawk will let go the one she has caught in her endeavour to defend herself from her new antagonist, and the quarry will be lost ; the most that may happen is that the hawk will sustain serious damage. I have heard of a falcon having its eye pecked out at one of these assaults. Some falconers, among them Major Stanley Allen and Robert Spens, will not fly their hawks at crows. In these days, when riding to hawks is no longer possible on Salisbury Plain, it may take too long to get up in time to help a hawk in these circumstances.

In the old days when I used to see a lot of rook hawking with the late T. J. Mann and his hawks in Cambridgeshire, we never used to slip the hawks at a flock of rooks if there were any jackdaws among them. Jackdaws are much more active than rooks, and if a hawk picks out a jackdaw instead of a rook she will never catch it, and may have such a long flight that a lot of time will be wasted before she is taken down. However, on one occasion I took up a lost hawk on a jackdaw she had killed, and on which I found her feeding. No one saw the flight so I do not know the manner of it, but it was about two miles downwind from where she had been slipped at a flock of rooks. That was in 1894.

The hawk herself was a passage falcon of the previous year,

and a very good hawk. She gave many a fine exhibition of high-ringing flights. She was about the quickest one to get above rooks that I ever saw. On being thrown off at a rook, her tactics were immediately to take a long flight, either down or across wind close to the ground ; then turning and throwing herself into the wind would come back, mounting at a tremendous pace, and would very soon be above the rooks. Being also a fine " stooper " and a good " footer," she generally killed her rook. Her name was Stratagem.

Here is a note from my diary concerning an incident with a wild peregrine in the same year :

"*April* 5, 1894. To Chesterford with the hawks. Got four flights and four kills with Stratagem and Startaway As we were driving along the road on the lookout for rooks, we found a wild blue falcon waiting on high above us. We got out a live pigeon, and when she had turned round towards us we let the pigeon fly and the falcon came down in a splendid stoop, close shut in. But the pigeon made a fence just in time. The hawk seemed much annoyed and savage at having missed her stoop and proceeded to rake away, and made three (apparently) savage stoops at a couple of hares which took no notice of her. Probably she never meant to touch them, but was evidently much put out and must vent her spleen on something."

It is a fine sight to see a hawk that knows the game in all its intricacies forcing a flock of rooks into the wind until she can get the opportunity of a downwind stoop. Major Stanley Allen had a tiercel, Donegal, which pursued these tactics to perfection and nearly always caught his rook. But latterly he seemed to do so out of mere exuberance of spirits, and to enjoy the exercise of his power to do so, without appearing to want to catch one of them. He would force a flock high in the air upwind, then easily getting above them would stoop, scattering them all downwind, then rush them upwind again, and do the same thing time after time, until at last a clump of trees would become a refuge for the rooks and the hawk taken down to the lure.

Passage hawks and haggards have already had their wild experience in flying and killing quarry and have little to learn, whereas eyasses have to be taught everything. Of course, much of it comes naturally from heredity, but to start them on the road to being strong on the wing, and to learn to stoop and be active at turning, it is essential for them to be *hacked*. This means being kept at complete liberty from the time they are able to fly to the time they are able to kill food for themselves, when they must be

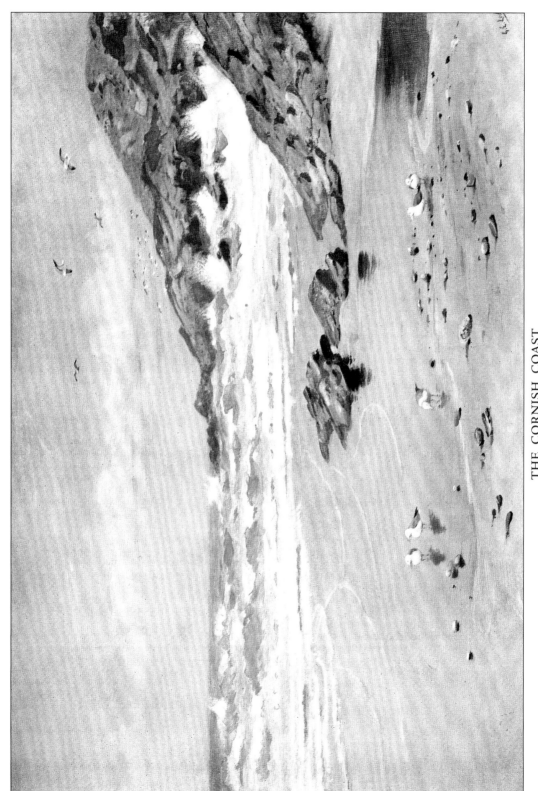

THE CORNISH COAST
A quiet cove near Mullion.

taken up at once for putting into training. Otherwise, they will undoubtedly stray away altogether. During this period they must be fed regularly at the hack house on boards, or on blocks just outside the hack house, the food being tied down so that the hawks cannot carry it away. One lump of food is given to each hawk being hacked. They can be kept at this for three or four weeks, or sometimes even longer. But one must be constantly vigilant to ensure the hawks coming in regularly for their food. If one is missing at feeding time it is generally a sign it is preying for itself, and on the first opportunity when it does appear the bird should be taken up, either with a bow-net set out in readiness or snared with a line on its block, which is done by the falconer from his hiding-place in the hut.

Food should be placed out for them early in the morning and in the evening. When the birds are first put out and quite young, three meals a day will be necessary, but after they are flying freely the two meals will be sufficient.

All this time that they are flying wild they will be getting strength and speed and will learn a certain amount of stooping, and achieve activity in turning as they play about together in the air. All eyasses should be hacked whether they are to be used for game or rooks. I have seen eyasses that have had no hack make most lamentable performances at rooks, having no enterprise at ringing up after a rook that takes the air, and making most clumsy stoops at any angle to the line of flight of the rook— missing by yards. Such hawks will certainly kill a few unenterprising rooks but will show very little sport.

Passage hawks are far away the best for rooks and a steady one cannot be beaten for game. But I have seen many an eyass flying and killing game as well as any passage hawk that ever flew. One of Blaine's eyass tiercels, Lundy III, made the following kills in the eight seasons 1907-1914 inclusive: 373 partridges, 106 grouse, 12 pigeons, 19 various—a total of 510 head.

Haggards are not so much in request for training purposes. Being older and having had so much more wild experience, they are less reliable and are apt to be soon lost. They *check* at anything that may take their fancy, often a long way off and flying it out of sight.

Mann had a very fine haggard falcon caught on passage at the huts at Valkenswaard in 1892. This was trained by his falconer Alfred Frost (brother of John Frost who was falconer to the Old Hawking Club) and entered to rooks in 1893. She was lost the first day she was flown at wild rooks. She flew magnificently, but the first rook at which she was slipped beat her at some trees and farm

B

buildings after a fine exhibition of much stooping by the hawk and clever shifting on the part of the rook. She was taken down to the lure and flown again later in the day. But instead of flying at the upwind flock she was slipped at, she caught sight of some other rooks a good way downwind and went tearing after these, which she flew almost out of sight. We could see the rooks putting in to some trees round a farm and we never saw the hawk again. Doubtless she went sailing away downwind looking for quarry which she would eventually find and kill.

In like manner, a haggard being put up after a point at grouse had been obtained would be mightily tempted, before the grouse had been flushed under her, to rake off and fly any chance curlew or plover that might catch her eye, and even if not lost in conse- quence would be useless as a steady hawk for grouse.

Eyass hawks of whatever species should never be taken from the nest too young or they will probably develop into screamers, and a screaming hawk is an abomination. They should be taken when they are just ready to leave the nest ; if just after they have left, so much the better, but with peregrines this may not be so easily done, for a fluttering young peregrine scrambling about a steep cliff face is not easily captured by a man dangling on a rope.

I think falconers will agree that the best and the highest-couraged hawks are those that are the best tempered and gentlest in their manners ; and these hawks often do not show themselves to best advantage when *weathering* on their blocks, but often sit in fluffy, dumped-up positions. I am of course alluding to hawks weathering on their blocks unhooded.

Peregrines kill their quarry quickly by biting through the neck and then begin to eat the head. A rook is a tough customer, but a grouse or partridge is easily killed. Merlins always grasp their quarry tightly round the neck with one foot and then proceed to bite into the head.

Peregrines vary considerably in their plumage, some being darker than others and much more heavily spotted and barred on the under surface. Others have more of the salmon-coloured tinge on the breast and lower parts of the body, and some— especially individuals from eyries at Hornhead, Co. Donegal— might almost be considered russet-breasted birds.

As a rule, falcons are darker and heavier marked than tiercels, but some falcons are almost dove-coloured above and pale cream- coloured below. Whatever colour they may be, the flank feathers are always liable to be tinged with grey in contrast to the creamy yellow colour of the rest of the under plumage. A young dark hawk will moult out into dark adult plumage and a light-coloured youngster will similarly moult into a light adult. Once moulted, the same type of plumage is kept through succeeding moults.

It seems well known that when one of a pair of breeding peregrines comes to grief, the survivor quickly finds another mate to help rear the family. This bare fact is copied from book to book, but we rarely get details. Is the habit restricted to one sex or common to both? At what stages of the breeding cycle can it happen? Will the surviving bird act thus before hatching or only when there are young at the eyrie? Most important of all, is the new bird always or necessarily an adult in breeding condition? It would be supposed there would be more unattached " red hawks " of the previous year than adult " blue hawks."

One imagines that a falcon with much incubated eggs would have no time to find a new tiercel to hunt food for her, or the eggs might suffer. Has a red peregrine ever been seen at an eyrie, and if so has it been assumed that peregrines breed in immature plumage? It would be much more reasonable to suppose such a bird was an annexed non-breeding hawk, taking the place of a lost adult. We are still waiting for definite information on the subject.

I have had few opportunities of watching peregrines at their breeding stations but on several occasions I have stayed with Philip Rickman, who has lived all his life on the coast and so is well acquainted with the habits of his local peregrines. They are frequently robbed by egg collectors, but some get off safely.

Philip Rickman and I watched a pair on several days of June 1932, taking our lunch with us and telescope, field-glasses and sketch books. The birds resented our intrusion at first, but soon took little notice of us, and would sit for hours at a time at their perches. The falcon was much more demonstrative than the tiercel and would fly out screaming when people walked past on the beach below. The falcon had a beautiful salmon-coloured breast, not particularly heavily marked. The tiercel was a dusky bird, remarkably so for a tiercel. I thought him a far finer flier than the falcon.

Now and then, in their cruises out to sea, the peregrines would stoop at the gulls below them, though I do not think the hawks meant to strike. The falcon stooped one day at a gull sitting on the edge of the cliff, but she threw away just before hitting it and the gull let out a squawk, fluttered its wings and stayed where it was.

Once a strange peregrine came from inland and was ignored by both residents, yet on another occasion the falcon left her perch and chased a stranger far overland, stooping at it many times.

The gulls, passing back and forth all day, sheered a little farther out to sea when passing the peregrines.  Homing pigeons were also constantly flying past, but we never saw the peregrines take the slightest notice of them.  From the remains of pigeons on top of the cliff, it was obvious that the peregrines preyed on them largely.  Probably they made their kills in the early mornings, for the birds were never away from their cliff when we went along. We often saw them feeding on remains of food stored on ledges of the cliff, and sometimes the falcon would fly out carrying the remains of quarry with her.

Rickman eventually saw one eyass about with the old ones. He also saw one of the parents make such a savage stoop at a jackdaw that was continually passing with food that the daw took a hasty refuge in a rabbit burrow.  It took a long and anxious look round when it came out and before taking flight.

I stayed with Rickman again in June of the following year, when this pair of peregrines had two eyasses on a ledge halfway up a 300-foot cliff.  They looked perfectly able to fly on the 15th, but they did not leave the ledge until the 20th, when we found them on the edge of the cliff top.  They were both falcons and could fly well.  During the day they would fly high and play with the old falcon for ten minutes at a time, but they appeared clumsy and floppy in flight compared with her grace.

We saw the tiercel bring food to the eyasses on their ledge before they flew. He dashed in, stayed only half a minute and left the food for the eyasses to tackle for themselves.  They seemed well supplied and were never very hungry.  Once we saw the falcon fly about the cliff and out to sea for a quarter of an hour, carrying a pigeon along with her.  When the eyasses had once left their ledge and could fly, they were very shy and would not allow us to approach them even as near as gunshot range.

Rickman at times saw the tiercel bringing food for the falcon, which came out to meet him, taking it from him and flying back to the cliff to eat it.  He has described it to me so vividly that I have ventured to make a small picture of the scene.  This habit is followed, probably, while the falcon is incubating.

Peregrines will prey on small birds as well as larger ones.  Once, while staying with Frank Wallace at Corrimony, I saw a tiercel stoop at something behind a cottage and come up again with a small bird like a sparrow or chaffinch in his foot.  He mounted high and three times dropped the bird, each time stooping a few feet and catching it again.  The third time he let it fall nearly a hundred feet before he took it up again.

Conversely, Mr R. A. H. Coombes, writing to me from Carnforth, Lancashire, in 1935, recounts the following anecdote :

" I heard recently of a wild peregrine bringing down a grey goose on a Solway marsh. . . . A fell shepherd I once knew saw a pair of peregrines bring down a goose from a flock that was migrating north in April and was passing close by the falcon's eyrie. He picked up the goose, which was still alive, but had a broken wing."

### The Hobby

When flying peregrines anywhere in the vicinity of hobbies (*Falco subbuteo subbuteo* L.), the latter will often leave their retreat and show themselves in the air. It was a fairly common occurrence while hawking round Avebury, near Marlborough, to see these lovely little falcons showing off their magnificent flying powers. So much was this a sure draw for the hobbies that at some later date Mr J. Mavrogordato made a special journey to try the experiment of catching a hobby by the well-known Indian process of catching wild hawks with the aid of a peregrine (or other species of hawk) to the back of which a series of horsehair nooses is attached. He took one of his trained peregrines and after fixing the nooses flew his hawk to the lure. A hobby soon turned up and started to mob and stoop at the peregrine. It soon found itself caught by the foot in one of the nooses and the two hawks came fluttering down to the ground.

Mavrogordato then ran in, and after releasing the hobby from the snare gave it at once its liberty. Not wanting the bird, he was satisfied in having proved his ability to catch English hobbies in the Indian fashion.

It is a pity hobbies should be as useless as kestrels for sporting purposes. They are splendid fliers and extremely beautiful little hawks in their general shape as well as coloration. Their wings are very long and narrow and when closed the ends of the primaries reach beyond the end of the tail. The secondaries are very short, and I have noticed that when the wings are closed the outer secondary coverts reach below the secondaries themselves. When flying, the hobby has rather the appearance of a very large swift, and its powers of flight are so great that it has been seen by authentic observers to chase and capture not only swallows but swifts. It feeds largely on insects as well as small birds.

As I said, the hobby is useless in the tame state and cannot be induced to hunt at all. The late E. B. Mitchell tried them and failed, and Dr H. O. Blanford has tried five of them, eyasses and haggards, and has been able to do no more than fly them to the lure. He lost them all flying them to the lure, and I imagine the reason was flying them too late in the autumn when the urge to migration would be upon them and they would take advantage of their liberty.

I am not inclined to believe that hobbies ever did provide sport in the way of flying and killing quarry, but were used only for " daring for larks." A hobby was flown over the fields in order to make the larks lie close and the larks were then caught by a net dragged over the fields. Not a very high-class sport, certainly, but in those days the results were doubtless more important than the means employed.

It is a well-known fact that peregrines will prey on the kestrel (*Falco tinnunculus tinnunculus* L.), the remains of this bird having been found at eyries. On one occasion, many years ago, when I was with the late T. J. Mann in Norfolk, one of his tiercels which had been lost for a few hours was taken up on a kestrel which he had caught and was eating. I have also heard of a trained peregrine catching a sparrow-hawk.

I once saw the curious sight of a peregrine and a kestrel in quite amicable company. This was at Avebury, Wiltshire, on 17th August 1934. I was with Dr Blanford at the time and he was feeding up his merlin after a kill when a wild peregrine flew past within gunshot, followed by a male kestrel a few feet away. These two hawks kept on their course till they were out of sight. There was no hint of mobbing.

It would seem to be a fact that birds and beasts know quite well whether their enemy is hunting or not. If hunting, they either hide or fly away ; otherwise, they have so little fear of consequences that they indulge in the mobbing habit. All kinds of birds will mob hawks on occasion and hawks will mob larger birds. Peregrines, for example, often mob the golden eagle, and kestrels mob the buzzard.

One frequently reads letters to the papers about some great fight between a hawk and a heron. I have little doubt these wonderful sights are nothing more than a hawk, very likely only a sparrow-hawk, mobbing the larger bird with no intent of inflicting bodily harm. Peregrines seem constantly annoyed at the sight of a raven and will stoop time after time, but the falcons must know quite well not to be so foolish as to try to strike, for Mr Corbie turns on his back at the last moment and presents his very considerable beak.

When flying a peregrine at rooks it often happens that as soon as the falcon is above the rooks, one member of the flock drops out and attempts to escape below. The falcon then stoops at this particular rook. The question arises whether the rook knows the falcon has already singled him from the others, or does the falcon choose the individual which happens to drop out? I am inclined to think the rook attempts escape because he has been chosen.

An American correspondent, Mr Cornelius F. McFadden, has sent to me a most interesting account of catching hawks on passage, these being the American peregrine or "duck-hawk"; and as Mr McFadden has kindly given me permission to quote his letter, I here give it. "As we can very easily catch passage and haggard falcons (peregrine) on certain islands off the Atlantic coast, we are really in a fair way of saving our local nesting duck-hawks. By deflating the tyres on our car we can race along a beach of very soft sand, spot a peregrine sitting on the ground, approach to within 100 or even 50 yards, stop car, get out away from bird, scoop out shallow pit and lie out in it, having partner toss sand over legs to waist, and put a piece of burlap over our head and shoulders, hold a pigeon on a 9-foot cord, have him drive car away about 500 yards, and the falcon will be on its way over to you before two minutes have passed (or else you do not get that particular bird). They fly over once trying to make our bait bird fly, and not succeeding, alight on the sand near you, cock their head, and stroll over, mute, and fly round again. This keeps up for two or three minutes, while you close your eyes, try to quiet your heart, and other such small jobs. Then one alights on ground, being fed up with the dumb pigeon not trying to save its life by flight, walks over and grabs it good and proper, and tugs in trying to pull it away. You have long ago pulled in the pigeon to your finger tips, having had to flick it to get a bit of action for the falcon's proper edification. Then reaching carefully around with your icy fingers (though it's really nice and warm in the hot sun), get one leg and have a fine time trying to find the other, knowing all the time that falcons do have two; finally find it, and attempt to sit up. You know then that the falcon is really annoyed. But we know of several instances where the same one has been taken twice in the same manner in the same day. After getting a proper sized hood on her, jesses and swivel, we wrap her up carefully in a piece of cloth, and start out for another one. I know of instances where twenty falcons and tercels have been taken in a single day, by three or four chaps teaming up this way. Mostly we size them up for color and stuff, band them, and let them go their way, taking but a pair home with us. I can tell you one (event) that I didn't see, but don't doubt the narrator. On catching a tercel and three or four looking at him and not thinking much of his color or some such nonsense, they tossed him off.  Someone at that moment lost a pigeon from his pocket, and the ensuing show by the same tercel nearly drove them crazy.  He took it within 40 yards of them, and not in the least disturbed by his recent experience or company, proceeded to pluck his quarry.  Amazed, one of the party walked over to him and slowly but surely actually touched his foot, and walked back to the amazed trio.  So he did it again to see if it was a fluke, and again had no trouble.  So then one of the party was wild to have that tercel, and the same chap started over to pick it up from the partly devoured pigeon—no dice—and no chances on that beauty ; so they put a knife into the ground, and walked round it with a cord snagging its feet and secured him (wound him up) and got him to fly free in three days ; but he wandered away over the hill within two weeks' time, never to be seen again, but keeping the bells and jesses to show his friends that might not believe his experiences. And that really happened the past Fall.''

I will conclude this section with the following notes on weights of peregrine falcons.  These weights are few in number, but they show considerable variation.

*Falcons* :  three trained falcons at Avebury, 1932, weighed hooded, 1 lb. 14 oz., 1 lb. 12½ oz., 1 lb. 11 oz.  An adult falcon shot at Docking, Norfolk, 1909, 2 lb. 2 oz.  A trained eyass falcon (intermewed), Black Jess, 1936, 1 lb. 6 oz. (very thin).  Immature falcon shot at Lissadell, Co. Sligo, rather fat, 2 lb. 7 oz.

*Tiercels* :  Avebury, 1933, four trained tiercels weighed, Midget (Bristol) 1 lb. 1¾ oz., Patrick (Irish) 1 lb. 4 oz., Satan 1 lb. 6 oz., Sir Umar 1 lb. 2 oz.  Two others weighed (Irish) 1 lb. 3½ oz., (Scottish) 1 lb. 5 oz.*

## II. Gyr-Falcons

There are four races of these magnificent birds, the gyr-falcon (*Falco rusticolus rusticolus* L.), the Iceland falcon (*Falco rusticolus islandus* Brünn), the Greenland falcon (*Falco rusticolus candicans* Gm.) and the Labrador falcon (*Falco rusticolus obsoletus* Gm.).  The Labrador falcon is darkest in coloration and markings and the Greenland falcon the lightest.  The individual variation is great and the plumage of the various races assimilates to such a degree

---

* At the present time (1944) the Government edict for the destruction of peregrines is no doubt necessary as a war-time measure, as peregrines play havoc with military carrier pigeons which may be bearing important messages and despatches.  But it is much to be hoped that as soon as the war is over the peregrine will once more take his place in the ranks of strictly preserved birds.

that it is often impossible to determine to which race a specimen may belong. It is impossible to reckon them as different species but only geographical races of the same one.

The description of typical examples of these races may be summed up as follows :

The Greenland gyr-falcon is a white bird. In its first plumage the feathers on back, scapulars and wing coverts are white with more or less large drop-shaped markings of a dark brown colour; the head is white with narrow, dark shaft streaks on crown and cheeks. The under parts are white, each feather with a dark, longitudinal central streak; the tail is white with dark bars across the feathers. Such a bird will moult white, all feathers on the upper parts with a blackish crescentic bar; head, tail and under parts entirely white, generally with very fine dark shaft streaks on crown, cheeks and flanks.

The Iceland gyr-falcon is a much darker bird. In first plumage all upper parts are dark brown, with light whitish edges to the feathers; under parts yellowish white with broad, dark longitudinal markings, getting larger and more V-shaped on flanks; head sometimes altogether dark, but often whitish with dark shaft streaks; tail dark with indistinct lighter bars. The adult plumage of this race is dark brownish grey on upper parts, barred across with light grey; under parts creamy white or quite white, streaked on the upper part of breast with narrow black shaft marks, these markings getting more pronounced into spots and arrow heads lower down, until at flanks they are broad black bars; head white with dark streaks in centre of each feather, in some cases the white predominating, in others the dark colour; tail barred with dark and light grey.

The gyr-falcon is very similar in its plumage to the Iceland bird, but is generally darker in both stages of plumage, especially the head, which is often almost completely black. The Labrador gyr-falcon is blacker still.

The gyr-falcon breeds in Norway, and the other subspecies in the countries after which they are named. All the same, both Labrador and Iceland birds breed in southern Greenland and the Norwegian type breeds sparingly in Iceland. These facts emphasize the difficulty of differentiating with certainty between the plumage of the various races. One can put a row of skins on a long bench with the whitest *candicans* at one end and the blackest *obsoletus* at the other, and merge from one to the other until at the middle of the row it is impossible to know whether the specimens are dark *candicans* or light *islandus*. This can be done with both immature and adult stages of plumages.

C

These falcons do not vary their plumages at successive moults, and the opinion of old-style ornithologists that they may get whiter as they grow older is without foundation.    I have an Iceland falcon in my collection that lived for nineteen years in the London Zoo, from March 1873 till April 1892, and this bird was still typical of the Iceland race, profusely spotted and barred in lower plumage and head, with more dark than light colour about it.    I have also several of the *candicans* race in their first plumage which are much whiter than most of my adult specimens.    One especially, reputed to be a Scottish bird, a male, has the whole of the head, under parts and tail pure white, the lower flank feathers only having very narrow dark shaft streaks.    This bird was originally in the late Robert Hargreaves' collection, and though I understood from him that he received the bird in the flesh, there are no data with the skin.

The other reputed Scottish specimen in my collection is an adult given to me by the late J. Maclean Marshall, who originally bought it, cased, from a shop in Edinburgh.    This bird is also without data.    It was badly mounted—as all gyr-falcons are— and when I came to take it down in order to remount it I found scraps of old newspaper inside, one bearing the legend " New Forth Bridge, Today (Monday) 25th May, 1896."    Two others from Co. Mayo, 1906, are males in immature plumage and almost as white as the Scottish bird.    They are very faintly shaft-streaked on head and flanks and one of them has an unmarked white tail ; the other has a few light brown broken marks at the centre of the two central tail feathers.

On the other hand, several of my adult birds are not only heavily marked on the upper plumage but have black-streaked heads, black-barred tails and a certain amount of flank and leg-feather marking.    One in particular, a male from Greenland, has the upper plumage marked with broad black crescentic bars, the head streaked black, tail barred with black even to the outside feathers which have unbroken bars.    The flanks and lower parts of the body are spotted with black at the subterminal end of each feather, these marks on a few of the longer (lower) flank feathers spreading out laterally into half bars.

It is not easy to have the opportunity of watching living gyr-falcons through successive moults, but on two occasions I have been able to do a little in this way.    They were both of the Greenland race.    One was a rather light, typically marked bird in first plumage, and I made careful sketches through three successive moults.    She first moulted into a rather unusual phase of plumage, all dark markings on the upper parts being in long, narrow, looped and

V-shaped markings. This style of plumage was retained. She even kept through these three moults four small dark markings on the right outside edge of one of the central tail feathers.

The other was also of Greenland type, caught in its immature plumage in Pembrokeshire and sent to the London Zoo. It was a very light bird with small markings and it moulted into an adult plumage with small markings, merely very small dark spots, lines and arrowheads. This I noted through four moults, though after the last the markings were slightly larger. The beaks of both these birds were always light blue and never became yellow.

The immature plumage of the white Greenland race can always be recognised by the markings of the back, scapular and wing coverts being longitudinally drop- or heart- or wedge-shaped and brown in colour  These markings in the adult are much blacker in colour, and whether large or small are more horizontal, tending to form cross bars.

It appears from explorers' reports that in the most northerly range of this falcon only the white race has been observed. *Candicans* seems to be a greater wanderer in winter than any of the other races. It is remarkable, considering the nearer proximity of Norway and Iceland. Only two authentic records of the Norwegian race have been recorded in the British Isles. A third example obtained at Hatfield Broad Oak, Essex, has been recorded in one book as being *rusticolus*, but I saw the bird and it was nothing but a dark female peregrine in immature plumage. This mistaken record has been put right in the new edition of Witherby's *Handbook of British Birds*, in which work will be found a most concise and comprehensive account of the gyr-falcons.

It has been definitely known that the Norwegian race, *F. r. rusticolus*, breeds in Iceland, and as far east as N.W. Russia. In 1936 the late Ernest Lewis (Vesey) went to Iceland to obtain eyass gyr-falcons for training. He returned with six, three being excessively dark birds and fine examples of the Norwegian race. Two of these are now in my collection. All the birds were delivered to G. Blaine in Islay to hack. One of them, a tiercel, was accidentally drowned while at hack and Blaine very kindly sent it to me.

This bird, in immature plumage, has the whole of the upper parts dark blackish brown, with paler brown edges to the feathers; the head is blackish brown with light streaks on forehead and light edges to feathers in centre of back of crown, back of neck and sides of crown from the eye backwards; the cheeks are streaked whitish and black; the whole of the under parts are heavily streaked with broad, blackish longitudinal streaks, the flank feathers having more black than white on them. Even the chin feathers are streaked with black. The tail is blackish with narrow lighter half bars.

The other bird of Vesey's which I have is a falcon in adult plumage. This bird ultimately found its way to the London Zoo, where it died in February 1939. It had therefore gone through two moults and is a very handsome dark example of a typical Norway falcon. The light markings on its upper plumage are very small and it is heavily spotted and barred below. This falcon is referred to as " The Gorgon " in Vesey's most interesting book, *In Search of the Gyr-Falcon*, written under his pseudonym of Ernest Lewis.

In some exceptional cases the light markings on the upper plumage of immature birds are salmon colour instead of being white. I have an example of this phase in an immature *F. r. candicans* from Greenland. All the light ground colour of the upper plumage is pale yellowish white, deepening to salmon colour on primaries, secondaries and primary coverts. This is a heavily marked bird with striped head and breast and barred tail.

Another bird in the national collection from S.W. Greenland is of *F. r. islandus* type. It has a white black-streaked head and all the light markings on the dark brown feathers of the upper plumage are bright salmon colour.

A bird in my collection has a remarkable mixture of plumage, being a patchwork of *islandus* and *candicans*. It is an immature bird from Greenland and came from the Schiøler collection, and was sent to me labelled *Falco rusticolus islandus*. The head is white, streaked with brown, and under parts white, rather broadly streaked with brown. The primary feathers of the left wing are typical of *islandus*, being dark brown with white tips, broken freckled whitish spots on outer webs and barred and freckled on inner webs. The right wing has much whiter primaries, some feathers being white with dark tips and bars across the outer webs like *F. r. candicans*. The secondaries and secondary coverts on both wings are mostly white, cross-barred dark as in *candicans*, but two secondaries on each wing (not corresponding feathers) are dark with freckled light cross bars like *F. r. islandus*. The scapulars, wing-coverts and back are a mixture of the two races, some feathers being white and others dark. The tail has every one of twelve feathers different. Those on the left are mostly white, one entirely so except for a small amount of dark freckling on the inner web. The other feathers on this side have some freckling on the outer web as well. The two central tail feathers are white on one web with a certain amount of dark, broken, more or less longitudinal markings and frecklings, the other web being altogether dark with light freckled bars across. One of the feathers on the right side of the tail is almost entirely *islandus* type, dark with light cross bars on both webs. Other feathers are mostly dark with light bars on the inner web, and white with broken dark markings, some tending to a longitudinal direction, broken into cross bars on the outer web. It would have been interesting to have this bird alive and have seen how it moulted.

I have photos of two gyr-falcons which were lifted at the same time from one eyrie, though I do not know in what country the eyrie was. One of these photos shows the two birds in immature plumage on their blocks. One bird is a very dark heavily marked typical *F. r. rusticolus*, the other is a typical *F. r. candicans*, of the strongly marked kind.

Both these birds moulted out and I have photos of the *candicans* which is absolutely typical of this race. I have no photo of the other bird in its adult plumage, but I saw it alive and it had no trace of anything but *rusticolus* about it.

There is no reason why, in a place like Iceland, the two types should not interbreed occasionally and the types would tend to segregate out in later generations.

There are other races of gyr-falcons, but they are so rare in collections and so little is known of them in their wild state that I can do little but mention their names here. Lorenz's gyr-falcon, *Falco lorenzi* (Menzb.), I have only seen once, when I figured a specimen many years ago for Menzbier's *Monograph of the Gyr-Falcons* (which book I have never seen !). My recollection of it is that it is precisely like *F. r. islandus*, but the margins of the upper plumage had reddish-coloured edges.

I think there is one specimen of the Altai gyr-falcon, *Falco altaicus* (Menzb.), in the national collection. This is a much browner bird than the other gyr-falcons and is heavily streaked with dark brown on its lower plumage. It is not so much spotted and barred as the others.

The Shanghar falcon, *Falco cherrug milvipes* Jerdon, is a red-coloured bird, with dark cross bars, very like a hen kestrel in colour and pattern of plumage, but with not so many cross bars on the tail. In its immature plumage it is brown with rusty red edges to the feathers on the upper surface, and the feathers on the lower surface are streaked with dark brown on a reddish buff-coloured ground. These several eastern races inhabit Siberia, Central Asia, Afghanistan and Tibet and appear to have been seldom found farther west.

In olden days the gyr-falcons seem to have been in much greater repute for falconry than in modern times, but there are scant records of what they were capable of doing or what they did. In England they were used for kite and heron hawking at the time when kites were common and herons on passage from their feeding grounds to the heronries were regularly flown by trained hawks. For herons, however, a cast of peregrines (falcons) were usually used.

A good many gyr-falcons were brought to England in the middle and early part of last century, mostly eyasses from Norway and Iceland, but few seem to have survived the climate and those few rarely caught wild quarry. Two or three turned out to be really good rook hawks. We never hear of them having been used for game. Whether they were ever trained to wait on for this purpose we do not know. Neither do we know if this form of sport had ever been tried and given up because the gyr-falcons were unsuitable. There are no records of what races of these falcons were used, though it is vaguely understood or said that *candicans* was the least satisfactory and *rusticolus* the best.

From the little that has been done in modern times with gyr-falcons it seems they are unsuitable for game hawking, being too unsteady to wait on patiently. But so few have been tried that it is hardly fair to dogmatise. You may try several peregrines before you get a good one. For every gyr-falcon trained there must have been many hundreds of peregrines.

There is a lack of big enough quarry for gyr-falcons in this country. They are wasted on grouse and partridges, which peregrines manage to perfection. The only things left are wild geese, blackcocks, mallards and cock pheasants. There are not so many places where a flight at wild geese could be obtained regularly.

It is on record that one of the Barrs tried this flight, and his experience was that the hawk would fly up to the geese but would refuse to tackle such a big quarry when it got there. We do not know how many hawks he tried or what race they were.

With the other quarry mentioned it would probably be better to fly the hawk *out of the hood*, as one does peregrines at rooks, rather than to have the hawk waiting on before flushing the quarry, as is done in game hawking. It is not always easy to know whether you have a blackcock or a cock pheasant waiting to be flushed under a waiting-on hawk. If you are working with dogs you do not know for a certainty at what a dog is pointing, and without dogs a walked-up blackcock will never alight again within sight if flushed before the hawk is waiting on. In all probability the best chance would be to have the hooded hawk on your fist, ready to slip at a blackcock when flushed. Unfortunately, blackcocks are never numerous enough to be certain of being found in suitable country for flying a hawk.

I am under the impression that tiercels might make good rook hawks. They are very fast and would probably get up to their rooks quicker than a peregrine. A rook is a very active and shifty quarry, and I think only tiercels would be able to cope with them. A falcon with her wide spread of wing would not be quick enough. Both tiercels and falcons might be very good for gulls.

The only gyr-falcon I have ever seen trained to wait on and fly at game was one of those the late Ernest Vesey brought back from his expedition to Iceland in 1936. This hawk, a tiercel, was hacked with the others by Gilbert Blaine in Islay, and it was there I saw the capabilities of this bird as a game hawk in the following season.

This gyr-falcon was a typical young *islandus*, very different from the dark *rusticolus* birds previously described. It was undoubtedly a magnificent flier and was, on the whole, very quiet and good tempered. But he was independent on the wing and nothing would induce him to wait on steadily overhead like a peregrine ; we were continually luring him up from a distance. And he had a habit of seeming very slow at making up his mind about stooping when a quarry was flushed. Also, he would not finish his stoop at low-flying quarry, but would *throw up* before he was within feet of it as if he were afraid of hitting the ground. He would mount to a tremendous height on fine sunny days, but in a wind he would not get up at all. Once he did make up his mind his pace and stoop were tremendous and he had no difficulty in overtaking a quarry that had got a very long start.

I saw him kill a cock pheasant while I was there, some hen pheasants and several grey hens. He took these last with the greatest of ease, trussing them and carrying them a little way before coming to ground. I saw him fly only one blackcock, and as the sequel was rather amusing—although vexing—I will quote from my diary :

"*September* 24, 1936. Hawking in afternoon : some rain. We tried the setters over some rough grassy places in hopes of finding either black-game or pheasants. Getting a point, the gyr was put up, but he would not get up, only cruising about close to the ground. We went in to the point and an old blackcock got up. The gyr was, as usual, a good bit wide, but he gave chase and we saw him take stand on a telephone post on the roadside some distance off. When we got there we searched about with the spaniel Cora in the small ditches and heather by the roadside, but our search was in vain.   This was on the march of Blaine's land which just here is cut into by a piece of land owned by a neighbour. Presently we saw this fellow about 200 yards off, hunting with a retriever about the ditch which ran at right angles to the road, into his property.   We saw him take the blackcock (he had evidently seen the *put in*) and go off home with it."

Another day while I was there he was lost.   He was put up after a point and a hen pheasant was flushed.   This he flew after a fashion and left, took the air, mounted to a tremendous height and soared away out of sight.   We spent the rest of the morning hunting downwind for him, without success.   Again in the evening (after having flown the peregrines and killed a brace of grouse) we stayed out until nearly dark searching and luring for him.   It was a bright sunny day and all the hawks flew very high.

Next day, in the afternoon, when one of the peregrines had just been taken down to the lure after an unsuccessful flight, the lost gyr suddenly turned up from nowhere and sat on the ground alongside us.   He was evidently very hungry and had probably not killed for himself since he was lost.   Blaine took him up on a lure.   One peculiarity of this bird was that he would allow only Blaine to take him up in the field, either on quarry or lure, although Blaine's falconer, Leonard Potter, always attended to him and fed him on days he was not flown.

This hawk was lost after I left.   He had flown a covey of grouse, killed one a mile away and was not found until nearly dark, by which time he had eaten the grouse and then refused to be taken up.   He flew away and was never seen again.   It will be seen, then, that this individual was no unqualified success as a game hawk.

It was fine to watch and admire his splendid flying powers, but much more than that is required in a good game hawk.   He was too independent and too little amenable to the lure.   Doubtless good sport could have been had with him if blackcock had been plentiful enough to have ensured a flight when desired and to have flown him direct out of the hood.   Grey hens and hen pheasants were much too easy for him.

I have no personal experience of gyr-falcons in a wild state, having seen only three in my life, two of the *candicans* race soaring together in South Sweden, and one young *rusticolus* tiercel which flew past me in northern Norway near Hammerfest.

From all accounts they appear to feed on anything they can get, probably such birds as happen to be most numerous in the vicinity. Coastal birds doubtless prey largely on gulls and auks, and those further inland on ptarmigan, willow grouse and the smaller nesting

MERLIN, WITH YOUNG
Near Lerwick, Shetlands.  June 30, 1922.

waders. In parts of Greenland one learns that snow buntings and lemmings are taken by the *candicans* race. C. Dalgety has told me he found the remains of a white-fronted goose (probably the lesser white-fronted) in a gyr-falcon's eyrie in Finland from which he took an eyass.

Vesey records in his book, *In Search of the Gyr-Falcon*, that in his opinion the falcons in Iceland make their own nests, as he differentiates between the occupied nests he found there from the ravens' nests, of which he saw many. Wolley also seems to hold the same opinion of the falcons in Finland and Lapland, from what one gathers in *Ootheca Wolleyana*. This, if so, is a departure from the usual custom of falcons, which is either to lay their eggs on the bare surface of the chosen place or use the old nests of other birds, and these big northern falcons would probably take the old nests of ravens or rough-legged buzzards.

One of the most regretted things in my life is never having had the opportunity of studying the habits and life history of these beautiful falcons in the wild state.

### III.  THE MERLIN

Many memories come into my mind concerning the merlin (*Falco columbarius æsalon* Tunstall), some of wild birds and others of trained ones. Merlins are the easiest of all hawks to train, and give sport with larks and pipits. Wild merlins will feed on any kind of small bird that comes their way, but for testing the flying powers and getting the full benefit of a sporting flight, a quarry that takes to the air such as a lark or pipit is essential. A hunt close to the ground from bush to bush or along a hedgerow is more suitable for a sparrow-hawk. Sometimes a lark will go ringing into the sky in front of a merlin beyond human vision, and a good merlin will even then force it to the ground and take it.

The difference in tactics between a wild and a trained merlin is very noticeable. The former is so much quicker, especially in turning, that it is always close on to its quarry which it seems able to prevent going to ground or getting away high, until at last it is taken in the air. A trained merlin in pursuit of a ringing lark takes such wide rings as it mounts that much time is taken to close up to the quarry, get above it and put in a stoop. The lark is almost always forced down and taken either on the ground or just before it alights, and rarely taken in the sky. This is just as well from the falconer's point of view as the temptation to carry would be great, not from intent so much as just drifting on to find a suitable place to alight and break into its quarry. That is how hawks get lost.

D

Sometimes a wild hawk—sparrow-hawk, kestrel or hobby—will appear on the scene and join in the flight of a trained one. An excellent merlin called Girl Pat, owned and trained by Dr H. O. Blanford, was hard after a lark high in the sky in North Cornwall, when a wild blue peregrine tiercel suddenly appeared and seized the unfortunate lark in front, and within a few feet of the merlin. But before he could fly off with his small quarry the excited little merlin grabbed the peregrine and they all came fluttering to the ground together. We ran up, greatly afraid that Girl Pat would be damaged or even carried off by the peregrine, but luckily this did not happen. The peregrine went off with the lark and Girl Pat in the opposite direction.

Girl Pat was flying again on the evening of the same day and had just caught a lark close to the ground, when probably the same tiercel stooped at her. But the quick little merlin evaded him and yet another stoop until the aggressor was driven off by our shouting. After all this excitement she was perfectly amenable and allowed her owner to take her on hand as an ordinary matter, with her quarry still in her foot.

Merlins in their first plumage, and females when adult, are very similar in colour and markings to peregrines in first plumage; much more so than are hobbies, despite the oft-repeated saying in bird books that " the hobby is a miniature peregrine." A hobby is not like a peregrine.

An abnormally coloured merlin came under my observation a few years ago. It was abnormal in two respects : first, it was half albino and second, what coloured plumage it had was the fully adult plumage of a male merlin, although it was a bird of the year and so had never moulted. It was taken from a nest in Yorkshire in which it was the only abnormally coloured one.

Another youngster in this nest had whitish-coloured claws. The bird came into the possession of Kim Muir, who let me have it for a week in order to take as many sketches as I wanted. I ultimately painted a life-sized portrait of it sitting on its block.

The nest of young merlins in the illustration was done from a pencil sketch made in the Shetlands on 30th June 1922. It was about four miles from Lerwick, situated on a steep heathery bank sloping up from a little burn. The nest itself had been a hooded crow's. There were five young ones, but the fifth could not be shown in the sketch as it had wandered a little too far away. Only one of the youngsters was in the nest itself and all the time they were being sketched—about half-an-hour—not one of them moved at all. The parent merlins soon appeared, the hen first, and mobbed around screaming all the time we were there. There was no trace of food round the nest, not even a feather.

Merlins usually nest in heather on the ground, but occasionally vary the site and make use of rocks and old nests in trees. James Hay, the watcher on North Roe in the Shetlands, showed us a ledge about halfway up a small vertical bank of rocks about 20 feet high where merlins had nested the previous year. I have also seen merlins occupying an old carrion crow's nest in a thorn bush on a grouse moor in Shropshire.

The merlin breeds in the moorland districts of Britain, but after the nesting time it is fairly frequently seen in the southern counties. It is also known to breed on Exmoor.

Merlins will mob human beings sometimes, although not in the nesting season. I have had two such experiences, one in northern Norway on 19th August 1916, the other at Camberley, Surrey, on 8th March 1922.

Their food is mostly small birds and some insects. I once found a merlin eating a dragon-fly when I was in Norway in 1900.

The question has often been discussed by falconers whether a merlin is capable of catching a snipe. Dr Blanford had a merlin which killed two snipe at Longhope in the Orkneys in 1937. They were easy flights and gave little sport as the snipe were flushed at close quarters, and as both went to ground because the hawk was so instantly after them, they were taken there at once. But it is doubtful if even a wild merlin is capable of coming to terms with such a rapid quarry if it once takes the air. A snipe would mount far quicker than a merlin.

This merlin of Dr Blanford's was a very good flier and good at returning to the lure after an unsuccessful flight, but she was an inveterate and horrible screamer. She not only screamed while feeding or being approached at the block, but the whole time she was on hand in the field. This is most unusual, but all five of that nestful were the same. They came from Yorkshire.

Falconers should beware of too light jesses for merlins. Jesses made from dogskin gloves for these small hawks are good; those made from kid gloves are too thin. They are very nice for the merlin to fly with but are soon bitten through by their sharp little bills—and merlins are perpetually biting their jesses.

Some falconers bell their merlins; others do not as they maintain bells handicap them when flying at wild quarry. It is a matter for individual preference, though I think it safer to bell them, because it is easier then to find the hawk if it has killed in thick herbage. Personally, I cannot hear a merlin's bell unless it is within a few feet of me, but some can hear them many yards away.

I was with Dr Blanford and the merlins in Cornwall when his hawk flew a lark which disappeared over the high bank of a lane with the merlin in close pursuit. When we got there we found the sides of the lane a dense tangle of brambles, blackthorn and so on. Everything was in full leaf and therefore very blind. Nothing was to be seen of our birds, but presently Blanford heard the tinkle of the hawk's bell and, tracking it, located it in the thickest part of the jungle. He had to crawl in like a badger and after a good many yards of struggling through thorn and briar came up with his merlin with her quarry in her foot. Had it not been for the bell she would undoubtedly have been lost for that day at least.

These high banks in Cornwall have proved the discomfiture of many a lark. Making for them as cover and disappearing over the far side, the quarry will drop to the ground even though it is bare of cover just at that point. Cover is but a few feet behind it in the shape of gorse, brambles and the like, the bank itself having momentarily broken the visual contact between hawk and quarry ; but the hawk is in such close pursuit that it is over the bank and on to its quarry before the latter has time to realise what is happening.

Too small a block should not be used for merlins for, when jumping to the ground, they may get their jesses crossed over the top of the block and hanging in this plight may damage themselves.

The simplest method of tying a hawk to its block is to have an iron ring through which the spike of the block is driven into the ground. The block itself is not jammed tight to the ground, but enough space left for the leash to be tied to the ring and for the latter to have free play. This removes the chance of the hawk getting wound up close to the block in her perambulations on the ground. This commonly happens on blocks which have no swivelling device, and no hawk ever has the sense to unwind herself. This applies to peregrines as well as to merlins—in fact to all hawks which are supplied with blocks, as opposed to bow perches which are usually provided only for the short-winged hawks, namely, goshawks and sparrow-hawks.

## IV. THE SPARROW-HAWK

Of all our British raptorial birds, the sparrow-hawk (*Accipiter nisus nisus* L.) must be considered the most destructive to our small bird life, for this species feeds almost entirely on birds. It is relatively common in almost every district and must be responsible for an enormous annual toll, particularly of blackbirds. The young of game birds and fully grown partridges are also taken.

Kestrels, as is well known, feed largely on mice and voles and also on insects. In 1896 I found a considerable number of cater-pillars of a noctuid moth in the stomach of a male kestrel shot at Friskney in Lincolnshire. Another, shot at Woodhall Spa, Lincolnshire, in 1898, had its stomach crammed with beetles as well as a small casting of fur and tiny bones.

A rough-legged buzzard (*Buteo lagopus lagopus* Pontoppidan) which I found hanging up in a poulterer's shop in Holborn in 1888 had its stomach full of the remains of five mice or voles. The skulls among the mass of fur and bones told me the number. Another rough-legged buzzard shot in Sussex in 1919 had the remains of a small rabbit in its stomach.

A common buzzard (*Buteo buteo buteo* L.) shot in Lincolnshire in 1893 had been feeding on earthworms, and another shot in Scotland in 1904 had in its stomach a small casting in which were fur, a small frog's foot and some fish scales.

The sparrow-hawk is a bold and courageous bird, and the female will prey at times on birds much heavier than herself, even wood-pigeons. I have weighed hen sparrow-hawks from 8 to 9½ oz. and woodpigeons from 16 to 20 oz., and I have also weighed partridges from 11½ to 17 oz. So this hawk must be a very powerful bird to tackle and hold such heavy quarry.

A Sussex keeper of my acquaintance told me in September 1925 that he had just had a good view of a sparrow-hawk catching a partridge. He was watching a covey over a hedge when the hawk dashed over the hedge into the covey, which immediately took wing. The hawk failed twice to catch one and succeeded the third time. He caught the sparrow-hawk by frightening her off and laying traps round the dead partridge. I saw this hawk, which was one of the handsome heavily and darkly barred variety, with blackish upper plumage and inconspicuous red edges to the feathers.

The same keeper told me in 1919 that he had trapped forty sparrow-hawks in the previous season, which shows how numerous they must have been. About half of them had been trapped at bait not of their own killing. His plan was to shoot a woodpigeon, open it a little, scatter a few feathers to make it conspicuous, peg it down and plant a few twigs round, leaving an opening in the circle of twigs for the trap. Both cocks and hens were caught this way.

The same keeper was employed by his master to catch a hen sparrow-hawk on its nest as he wanted a haggard to train. He caught her in a muffled gin trap at the third attempt, the trap being too heavily muffled on the first and second occasions. There were three eggs in the nest. I saw this bird in September of the same

year, 1925, and found her to be something over a year old, still
in her first plumage but with a fair amount of new feathering,
especially on the secondary coverts.

She was quite tame and well " manned " and came to hand well
—as far as 150 yards from hand to hand. She would try to carry
anything given her on a string. I have always heard this habit
of carrying is not to be eradicated from haggard sparrow-hawks,
and for this reason alone I should consider them not worth bothering
about. The only thing to do would be to fly them at quarry too
heavy to carry. They could never catch a woodpigeon in the
open, and waterhens are too easy and give nothing of a flight.
A female sparrow-hawk could take partridges early in the season,
but later the partridges would get up so wild that the hawk could
not overtake them. A sparrow-hawk is very fast for a short sprint,
though it should be remembered this bird depends largely on
surprise at close quarters.

Sparrow-hawks build their own nests, unlike the true falcons.
The trees most generally chosen are larches and oaks. I have
seen one in an apple-tree in an orchard near Cambridge and,
unusually, it was built on an outlying branch. The nests vary much
in size, and some in larches can be very conspicuous, but a small
nest in the fork of an oak may be easily overlooked.

A tree alongside a ride is often chosen in preference to the
depths of a wood. Though so secretive in its habits, this hawk
will sometimes boldly choose the neighbourhood of a house. One
I knew in a cypress was only thirty yards from the house and
children hung a hammock from the tree and made the shelter
below into a playground. Another was in the grounds of a hotel
at Woodhall Spa where there was constant passage of people.

As a rule sparrow-hawks are not demonstrative when the nest
is disturbed by human beings, but one can hear their cry as they
fly around at a little distance. I have had one experience of more
aggressive behaviour—in June 1914, when I was up an oak tree at
Rotherfield, Sussex, making a sketch of the nest which contained
five newly-hatched young and one addled egg. One of the parent
hawks repeatedly dashed close past me, always coming horizontally
and almost touching me every time. As far as I could see, the
hawk settled on the branch of a neighbouring tree for a short time
after every assault. It came so quickly and the foliage was so
thick that I could never tell whether it was the cock or hen, but
I am inclined to think it was the cock as I should probably have
got more of an impression of size had it been the hen. My note
made at the time finishes, " I do not think it actually touched me."

It is quite certain sparrow-hawks breed in the year after they

SPARROW-HAWK, WITH NEST AND EGGS
Hartlebury, Worcestershire.  May 2, 1909.

are hatched, *i.e.* before they are a full year old and before they have moulted into their adult plumage. I got a hen from a nest at Woodhall Spa in 1919, which was in its first year's juvenile plumage and well in moult. She had only four primaries of the first plumage in each wing, these being the outside ones. From the appearance of the six pairs of new primaries they seemed to have been cast from the tenth in order outwards. Nearly all the secondary coverts were new and a good sprinkling of new feathers were coming in on the back and scapulars, but these feathers had not yet reached the surface of the plumage. The centre pair of tail feathers were cast and the new ones were just coming down. I could find no traces of new feathers on the rest of the body.

The keeper who got the bird for me said he had found that all sparrow-hawks he had shot at the nest were in moult, so presumably adults as well as immature birds are affected.

Like all the raptorial birds, the hen sparrow-hawk is larger than the cock, sometimes considerably so. On the other hand, it is sometimes surprisingly difficult to know whether you have a small sparrow-hawk or a large " musket," and I have noticed the same thing with goshawks.

I once had three freshly caught female sparrow-hawks sent to me from Lincolnshire (2nd February 1900). They had been caught in a large wire woodpigeon trap in a wood. One was a haggard and the other two in their first plumage. I had to straighten out their wing and tail feathers in boiling water as they were bent and then I put jesses on them. I was astonished how quietly they allowed me to do this until I remembered it was night-time and lamp-light. Each one lay quiet in my left hand while I manipulated the jesses with my right. After this I made them all feed on a partridge on my hand, which they did fairly readily. I put them on a screen perch for the night and found they would sit on my hand and feed quite well when I came to them next day.

The haggard was the best tempered and allowed me to stroke her breast on the second day while she was feeding. The other two bit my fingers if I put them anywhere near them. I sent the haggard to the late E. B. Mitchell a few days afterwards. He wrote back saying it was a musket, and asking for a musket's tail as he wanted to *imp* some tail feathers. I sent him tails of both male and female sparrow-hawks for this purpose, but the feathers of the female were too large and those of the male too small for the bird sent. This bird was lost during training so I still do not know whether it was a male or a female. Of the two others I sent one to the late R. Gardner and one I " let down the wind " as some of its feathers were too much broken for it to have been any good.

In training and manning a sparrow-hawk a great deal of patience and good temper is required, for in the early stages of the process it seems as if the inherent wildness of the bird will never be overcome. But man's will, given the patience and good temper, can prevail and the result will be a perfectly docile and tractable bird which will give plenty of sport with blackbirds and other small birds along hedgerows and root fields.

If a sparrow-hawk is unreasonably bad in learning to fly to the fist (as it should always be trained to do) or to the lure, a single night of being kept without sleep will work wonders. A hawk that would not come more than a few feet may be found to come readily twenty or thirty yards.

Sparrow-hawks are attractive if they are properly manned and given fairly plentiful exercise at wild quarry. They should also be carried a good deal. They do not seem ever to become as tame and faithful as merlins. They are delicate birds, liable to fits which usually prove fatal, and great care should be taken with their food, which should consist as much as possible of small birds, *e.g.* sparrow and starlings. Chickens' necks and sheeps' hearts are good food also, the former for all hawks and the latter for sparrow-hawks and merlins.

I have only once personally known a sparrow-hawk kept long enough to moult into adult plumage. This was a handsome and very good female owned and trained by J. Mavrogordato. She turned from the dark, heavily barred type to the common adult female plumage. There is little variation among adult female sparrow-hawks, but much among males. Thus, the variation which occurs in immature peregrines and is carried forward into adult plumage does not hold good for female sparrow-hawks.

There is one peculiarity about the plumage of European sparrow-hawks which was pointed out to me some years ago by Major Allan Brooks, the painter of American birds : that they are the only species of hawk to have a barred type of plumage of the under-parts in the juvenile state. Even the closely allied American sharp-shinned hawk (*Accipiter velox velox* Wilson) and Cooper's hawk (*Accipiter cooperi* Bonaparte) are streaked longitudinally on the underparts and do not attain the horizontally barred plumage until the first moult. The American goshawk (*Accipiter gentilis atricapillus* Wilson) in its first plumage is not to be distinguished from the European species (*Accipiter gentilis gentilis* L.), but when adult it is quite different.

In that excellent book *Ornithological Rambles in Sussex*, by A. E. Knox, published in 1849, there is a long and graphic account of the author's own experience of the depredations of one pair of sparrow-hawks during the summer of 1842. Being informed by his keeper that young pheasants were being taken from the coops, he gave instructions for a wood to be searched for the sparrow-hawk's nest. This was duly found in a thick oak tree, though the young birds had left it and were in a tree nearby. The nest itself was being used as a feeding place and was a well-stocked larder. To quote from the book : " . . . here he shook out upon the grass for my inspection the contents of the bag—there were fifteen young pheasants, about the size of quails—some rather larger—four young partridges, five chickens, a bullfinch, two meadow pipits and two larks, all in a fresh state." The full number of this family of sparrow-hawks was destroyed.

The sparrow-hawk is credited by some people with occasionally having the habit of disguising its manner of flight with the object of so deceiving its prospective prey as to allow a close approach. This style of flight, which I have never seen myself, is described as being executed in a slow and rolling manner, quite different from its usual dashing and gliding. I have never heard of anyone describing a kill from such tactics, and it may be doubted whether there is any foundation for the belief, even if the fact of this kind of flight be granted. There is too much of this crediting animals with a human type of intelligence on slender anecdotal evidence. The gambolling of a stoat in the presence of birds like lapwings is another oft-repeated example of animal deceit when in search of prey, but I do not recall an authentic objective account of such gambolling having the reputed sequel.

## V. The Kite

The European kite (*Milvus milvus milvus* L.) is by far the handsomest of the world's kites, unless it be the striking black and white swallow-tailed kite (*Elanoides forficatus forficatus* L.) of America. Unfortunately, our indigenous kites are now reduced to fewer than a dozen birds living in the wooded hills of mid-Wales. They were formerly so common as to appear as scavengers in the streets of London.

The kite on the wing when merely travelling looks very like a heron both in size and in the slow flapping of the wings. To appreciate its grace the bird must be seen soaring. Then his flight is very fine ; the long wings and forked tail show to perfection. The kite rises into the sky in circles on motionless wings, just tilting its body as it circles to get full advantage of air pressure, and ultimately disappears into the blue.

E

This I saw many a time in Sweden in 1882 and 1883, when they were fairly common over the lakes and woods. I was a keen collector at that time and shot three from a hide built in a little thicket of birches and sallows jutting out into the lake. I used dead bait in the shape of cats and the remains of a pig, which I found in a wood being devoured by crows and ravens.

The measurements of the first were 27 ins. in length and 5 ft. 3 ins. from tip to tip of outspread wings. It was loaded with fat and had the remains of a blackcock—probably what was left of some goshawk's kill—inside him. The second had very little fat, and was an inch shorter in length and 3 ins. shorter in spread of wing. Its crop and stomach were empty.

The third kite was also thin, its stomach containing only a partly digested small eel. At that time the local " hunting society " was giving as much as 4 kroner (1 kroner=1s. 1d.) for the legs of a goshawk—which was as much as they gave for a fox—and 2 kroner for sparrow-hawks ; crows were 25 ore (100 ore=1 kroner). But they gave no bounty either for kites or buzzards, thus showing that these birds were not considered inimical to game.

Kites are notorious for collecting all sorts of rubbish when nest building. Old rags and newspapers are common. While in Sweden I was told of a nest at the top of a very tall tree which was reached by a schoolboy. The inside of the nest was composed of an old waistcoat and two dead kittens were laid there. One egg had hatched and the boy brought the other down with him, but when he reached the ground he found this one had hatched also !

Many years ago, in the seventies of last century, I was at the Lincoln School of Art and made the acquaintance of an old taxidermist called George Adrian. I was vastly entertained by his stories of experiences with birds and beasts. He used to take kites' eggs in the woods near Lincoln and also collect kites with his gun. His method of getting the kites was to hide himself in a hollow willow tree with his gun, having previously tethered a dead rabbit with a string, letting it float on the water. He also told me that in the same woods he used to hunt pine martens with a dog—shooting them when he got the chance, which was usually when they were up a tree. I got from this old fellow the only specimen of a convolvulus hawk moth I have ever been able to collect. Years afterwards I found that Wooley of *Ooetheca Wooleyana* had several of the kites' eggs in his collection from George Adrian of Lincoln.

An abortive attempt was once made to increase the diminishing number of Welsh kites by introducing fresh blood in the shape of two young kites from Spain. These birds were so fearless and tame

KITE, WITH NEST
S. Wales.  July 5, 1921.

that they would have had little chance of escaping human hostility, so they were caught up again and after some years ended their days in the London Zoo.

The best way to get some fresh kites would be to put some clutches of continental kites' eggs in buzzards' nests, as these birds are common in the kite country. Admittedly, such a scheme needs a lot of organization.

The only personal acquaintance I have with the kites in Wales is contained in the following note from my journal :

"*July* 5, 1921. Meade-Waldo and I staying with Rev. Edmonds Evans to see the success or failure of the kites nesting in the neighbourhood. Some few youngsters have got off. One pair seems to have disappeared, but there is so much heavily wooded country for many miles and it is so wild and remote that there may be kites about without many people being the wiser. We have seen only two nests, from one of which two young had flown two days before our visit. We had a fine view of one of the old birds which circled above the nest for about five minutes, crying a double note, half whistle, half mew, not unlike a buzzard's note. There were many moulted feathers scattered about under the trees in the neighbourhood of the nest, tail feathers and secondaries, as well as contour feathers, so a complete moult was taking place.

" The other nest had come to grief and the birds had deserted. The watcher thinks this failure due to a photographer who had permission to visit the nest. The old birds were so shy that they did not return to the nest for several hours after the photographer had left, and in that time the eggs may have been raided by crows. It was evident that no one had been up to the nest.

" Both nests were in similar situations, about halfway up medium-sized oaks, and set against the trunk of the tree. The woods here are composed almost entirely of such trees. The nests are not large but very ragged. From a little higher up the hillside I could look down into the nest with my field-glasses and see lumps of sheep's wool in it. Close by one of the nests (the deserted one) was another nest of the previous year from which the young birds successfully flew."

I have two clutches of Welsh kites' eggs in my collection. The clutch of two was given me by the late E. G. B. Meade-Waldo, together with a letter from the watcher, who explained that these eggs had not been hatched by the birds that spring, and he compared with this fact the very poor hatching season among chickens. There had been three eggs in the nest and the one which hatched grew into a fine young bird. The second clutch is a three given to me by C. B. Horsburgh, with the data " Collector C. G. Carmarthenshire, S. Wales. 16 April, 1882. Set 3." I think this would be before any legislation for bird protection was enacted, with the exception perhaps of the Sea Birds Protection Act, which was designed to put a stop to the cruel and iniquitous practice of boat parties shooting indiscriminately every gull, puffin and so on that passed their way.

## VI.  EAGLES AND OSPREYS

The golden eagle (*Aquila chrysaëtus chrysaëtus* L.) is still fairly numerous in the Highlands of Scotland, but the white-tailed eagle *Haliætus albicilla* L.) is no longer a resident breeding species in Britain.  One or two stragglers are seen almost every year ;  they are probably Norwegian birds on passage.  The last resident example of this fine bird was an albino specimen which lived on North Roe, one of the Shetland Islands, for about thirty years. Originally it had a normal-coloured mate, and bred for the last time in 1908.  They generally used the same nest year after year, but at one time, Meade-Waldo told me, they had another nesting site on the island.  He remembered seeing the nest but at that time it was occupied by a pair of peregrines.  My personal experiences of this eagle are given from my diary :

"*June* 28, 1914.  North Roe.  Meade-Waldo, Ogilvie-Grant and self, with James Hay the watcher, went to where the sea eagle lives.  We saw her from a long way off, like a white spot on the cliff below the old nest which is still there on a 500-foot cliff.

" She was very wild and flew off and away and we did not see her again.  She is quite white and looks as white as a gull while flying.  This shelter was a big crack or chimney, with a split in the side opposite the entrance, from where we could look across to the nest which was about 100 feet from the top of the cliff.  I spent a time here making an oil sketch of the nesting cliff; but it was a horrid cramped position and a bad afternoon, blowing half a gale of wind and driving thick drizzling mist across.  I was fairly well sheltered and worked for one and a half hours, but was then too cold and cramped to continue so went home in the rain."

"*June* 30, 1914.  Very windy.  Went again to see the eagle. She was not in sight when we got there.  It was too windy to paint so I made a pencil sketch of the rock in the immediate vicinity of the nest.  While so engaged a hoodie crow continually mobbed something round the corner where we had no view, as it was shut in by the rocks on our left.  Meade-Waldo and Ogilvie-Grant therefore went out to the top of the cliffs to investigate, and out flew the eagle mobbed by two or three hoodies. I had a very short view of her as she passed across my crack opening at a distance of about a hundred yards. I noticed that her primaries were not white but appeared to be light brown. The nest seems to be a mass of rubbish and looks just like the surrounding rocks. We could see no trace of sticks, which lack would probably be due to wear and tear and stress of weather. However, I got material for a picture and the wild weather is eminently in keeping with the subject."

"*July* 10, 1922. North Roe. Meade-Waldo and I went for a long ramble with James Hay the watcher. We made for the Red Banks, the old nesting site of the albino sea eagle which has not been seen by Hay since 1918. On the way there we were bunkered by a burn in spate, up which we had to go for two miles before we could cross. We turned downstream again and went to the old place where I made the sketches in 1914. There is now not a vestige of the nest to be seen."

"*July* 13, 1922. Mr Ratter, the bird photographer at Lerwick, told us he had heard of a pair of sea eagles having been seen at two places in the Shetlands this spring, one of these places being Muckle Roe and the other Sandness, farther south on the west coast. He also introduced us to a young man whose father has seen two sea eagles at Ollaberry this year; also that he had heard that the old white sea eagle of the Red Banks was shot in 1918 by an old man. What had been done with the body he either could not or would not tell us. This date coincides with the time James Hay ceased to see anything of it."

Eagles are notoriously long-lived birds. As a case in point, Sir Herbert Maxwell told me in 1896 of a white-tailed eagle, a Scottish one, that he had known in captivity for forty years, and it was still well and healthy.

Here is a note from Norway recorded in my diary:

"*October* 4, 1899. Saw two sea eagles to-day on our way south before we got to Trondjhem. The first was flying a good height up, the second one flew in front of us and alighted on a little rocky island. It held its wings outstretched and highly elevated for about a quarter of a minute after alighting. As the steamer passed it flew off again and we had a good view of it surrounded by hooded crows which perched about the rocks within a few feet of it. If a crow ventured too close it shot out its wings, the wing on the side towards the crow being spread much wider than the other wing; and the crow would just slip off and settle again a few feet away."

One often sees golden eagles while stalking in Scotland. They are welcome in deer forests as they keep down blue hares and grouse which are so much of a nuisance to the stalker. All the same I have seen both single grouse and grey-hen, flushed during a stalk, fly past my quarry without causing undue alarm.

Eagles are not so popular when they get down from the high hills to the grouse moors proper, as they not only eat grouse, but the presence of an eagle will empty a whole drive of grouse. If it were not for the immunity they enjoy on the high ground they would soon be trapped out of existence.

I have a few notes in my diary on the subject of eagles attacking red deer :

" *May* 23, 1922.   Glencalvie, Ross-shire.   Macrae the keeper here tells me yarns about birds and beasts. He says he once saw a pair of eagles hunting a red deer calf, but he did not see the finish as they disappeared into wooded country. He also told me he saw through his telescope an eagle repeatedly stooping at a fox. He described it most graphically and went through the motions of the fox looking up with his head on one side, carefully watching the eagle's tactics, and leaping up at the eagle every time it stooped. He pointed to a hillside about half a mile off to show me the distance he was from them, and when I asked him whether he thought the eagle really intended to catch the fox, he said no, he did not think so."

" *September* 5, 1931.   Eilenreach, Inverness-shire.   A crofter by name Maclure came to the lodge and gave Percy Mann (my host) and me an account of an eagle he had seen carrying a red deer calf. He was droving cattle by the Eilenreach and Arnisdale march at the head of Aiodhalian on the evening of either 2nd or 3rd of June this year, and sat down for a rest (it being then about 9.0 p.m. B.S.T.) when he saw the eagle come flying down the slope with the calf in its claws. The eagle was about twenty feet above the ground and grasped the calf by the neck and shoulders so that the rest of the beast was dangling down. He estimated the calf to be about a week old and to weigh 12 to 14 lbs. This downhill flight lasted three hundred to four hundred yards and they came to ground about seventy yards from the observer. The calf began to squeal and the eagle gave a peck or two, but the old hind rushing madly down the hill caused the eagle to fly off. The calf lay still for two or three minutes, then got up and began to suckle its mother. The eagle flew round, about fifty yards up, and hovered for a short time before it flew off and was joined by two other eagles."

Golden eagles not infrequently nest in trees in Scotland, although rocks on steep hillsides are usually chosen as nesting

SEA EAGLE, MOBBED BY HOODED CROWS
Norway, N. of Trondjhem.  Oct. 4, 1899.

sites, these being in some instances easy to reach. As long as the site suits the bird it does not seem to heed whether there are branches all the way up or none at all until near the top. To get at some of these nests is as easy as walking up a ladder.

It is curious to see what unsuitable places to our eyes can be chosen as nests. On 9th May 1927 I went with Commander and Mrs Briggs to see an eagle's eyrie in Inverness-shire. We had fairly detailed instructions about the position, but we found it by rather a fluke as it was at the top of a small fir in a dense forest of much taller fir-trees on a hillside and it was revealed to us only by our noticing the dense top of this tree. By scrambling up a rocky bank we got level with the nest and could see into it from not more than twenty feet away. It was a huge mass of sticks, twenty feet above the ground, and contained two eggs, one freckled with red and the other plain white. The nest was flat with a central cup for the eggs. There were plenty of green fir shoots, heather tufts and dead grass in the structure of the nest. It was not worn much, though we had been told the eggs were due for hatching. No down or feathers, remains of food or excrement were to be seen, except that on the rock where we were the feathers of a grouse were found.

We saw no sign of the eagles while I was making a pencil sketch of the nest. It seemed deserted and there were the remains of a photographer's hide. Indeed, many weeks afterwards I was told these eggs were still in the nest. I still have no golden eagle's eggs in my collection.

Two years later I saw another golden eagle's nest in a fir-tree in the same vicinity. It was in a larger tree but not at the top. A nest on the Struy Forest which I saw in 1926 had plenty of remains of grouse, hares and rabbits round about, but it had not been occupied that year. It was on a steep, rocky hillside but easy to reach from below.

I have two weights of golden eagles to record, one an immature male, in perfect plumage but poor condition, trapped on Strathgartney, Perthshire, in 1913, weighed 5¾ lbs. The other, a male in adult plumage and very fat, weighed 9¾ lbs. Its wing spread was 6 ft. 6 ins.

The plumage of eagles is very subject to bleaching, which may give them a patchy appearance. This may occur to such an extent that at a distance they appear to have quite white patches on their wings. I have seen a letter written to one of the well-known weekly papers from a correspondent who claimed to have seen an imperial eagle in Scotland, this being identified by the white patches on the bird's shoulders. There is little doubt it was a golden eagle with a certain amount of bleached plumage. Stuffed specimens suffer terribly from this bleaching if exposed to the light, all the fine tawny colour of the back of the neck being reduced to a dull yellowish white. The only way to keep the colours of feathers of birds practically intact is to keep specimens as skins and stowed away in the dark in cabinets. But it is tempting and interesting to have some well-mounted specimens in cases.

Identification of wild birds should be received with the greatest caution. Under some conditions of light the appearance of a bird can be altered to an extraordinary degree. Rooks sometimes appear as black and white as a magpie when a strong sun shines on their polished plumage.

I once saw a bird at the top of a tree and it looked bright red in colour. Was it a cock crossbill? No, too large; and on closer approach I found it to be a redwing with a late afternoon sun bathing its plumage in a bright rosy light.

## The Osprey

There seems little doubt that the osprey (*Pandion haliætus haliætus* L.) has been cleared out as a breeding species in the British Isles by the depredations of egg collectors. From the time of St John onwards these beautiful birds have been shot at the nest and the eggs taken unmercifully.

Their favourite nesting sites were isolated rocks and old ruins of castles in some of the Scottish lochs. One or two pairs held their own until the turn of the century, but for forty years now we have had no breeding birds—or if we have had on rare occasions, the fact has had to be kept so quiet that few of us have had the pleasure of knowing it.

Every winter a few wandering migrants are seen in this country, especially about the Norfolk Broads, where Jim Vincent tells me that no winter goes by without his seeing an osprey at Hickling. I have seen ospreys in Norway, where I used to be E. Lort Phillips' guest, in the Sundal valley. I noticed there that while hovering, before plunging down at a fish, they hold themselves in a very upright position, flapping their wings rapidly. A fish is carried lengthways, head on, by which means there is least wind resistance.

I also saw an osprey in the West Indies; according to my notes: "*April* 23, 1896. Grenada. We visited by boat a pelican's roosting place. Also saw an osprey almost within gunshot, perching on a tree. He went off, plunged twice into the sea and flew straight away. We could not see whether he caught anything or not."

In 1907 I was in U.S.A., and while there spent three days with Frank Chapman on Gardiner's Island, as guests of Mr Gardiner, the proprietor of the island, which is some miles north of Long Island. Here there is, I suppose, the largest breeding colony of ospreys in the world. But we were there in November when all the ospreys were away in their southern winter quarters. The only one we saw was a dead youngster, fully feathered. There were many nests in all sorts of positions; some as large as haycocks were on the beach above high-water mark. Others were on fences and tree-tops, large and small. Most of them were on the tops of small dead trees; some of these trees had collapsed, probably aided by wind, from the weight of the nest on them.

*The Home-life of the Osprey*, by Clinton C. Abbott (Witherby), gives a full and most interesting description of this colony, together with numerous excellent photographs of the birds and their nests. The author says that two hundred nests would be a reasonable estimate. As evidence of the weight of an osprey's nest, he cites the fact of a " moderate-sized eyrie " that was transported from Gardiner's Island to the New York Zoological Park, as being over 400 lbs. Incidentally, while I was there with Dr Chapman, we saw the largest congregation of crows I have ever seen. It was evening and they were gathering before going into the woods to roost. They were first massing and settling on the fields with incessant cawings, then they left the ground and came along silently in what appeared to be never-ending streams. Dr Chapman estimated the number at somewhere about a hundred thousand.

The feathering on the upper surface of the wing of an osprey is in one respect different from that of any other bird I have examined. The six outer secondary coverts are considerably shorter than the other feathers of this row, and this shortness is compensated for by being augmented by six extra feathers growing from the same source, but which are larger and are much prolonged beyond the tips of the aforesaid shorter outer secondary coverts. I discovered this from an osprey I received in the flesh from the Zoo. Several careful drawings of the feathering of the wing were made, both of the upper and lower surfaces, before I mounted it.

# PART II

## WOODLAND AND MARSH

### I. The Short-eared Owl

ALTHOUGH the short-eared owl (*Asio flammeus flammeus* Pontoppidan) is a resident locally breeding species in the British Isles, the bulk of those seen in autumn and winter are foreign migrants, many of which come from northern countries. They are fairly often seen during shooting parties. Roosting on the ground, they are frequently flushed by beaters out of turnip fields while driving partridges; indeed, several may be seen in the air at one time. I have seen four of them come over the line of guns in Norfolk, and single ones many times, yet I have never seen one shot at. Being predatory largely on rodents there is good reason why they should not be shot.

These owls are more diurnal in their habits than most other species of this tribe, in this way their habits resembling those of the snowy, hawk and little owls (*Nyctea scandiaca* L., *Surnia ulula ulula* L. and *Athene noctua vidalii* A. E. Brehm). It is interesting to notice that these three owls all have light golden-coloured eyes, whereas the more strictly nocturnal species—when they do not have black eyes like the tawny owl (*Strix aluco sylvatica* Shaw) and the barn owl (*Tyto alba alba* Scop.)—have orange-coloured eyes like the eagle owl (*Bubo bubo bubo* L.), the long-eared owl (*Asio otus otus* L.) and the scops-owl (*Otus scops scops* L.).

The headquarters of the short-eared owl in the British Isles is in the Orkneys, but there are always some breeding in various parts of the kingdom in suitable localities like the Cheviot Hills, the Borders generally and the Norfolk Broads. There are always some at Hickling.

The nest is always on the ground among rough grass or sedge, and the old bird sits close on the nest while one inspects them for sketching purposes. It is impossible to know whether both sexes help in incubating the eggs as the plumages are indistinguishable. Presuming the hen bird is on the nest, the cock will sometimes mob the human intruder, flying around uttering its husky bark and then plunging down to the ground. I saw this happen on Sandy Island, Orkney, in July 1914, and my diary gives this note for a bird at Hickling:

42

SHORT-EARED OWL, WITH NEST
Hickling, Norfolk.  May 25, 1924.

"*May* 24, 1924. The cock bird made more of a demonstration here and presently plunged to the ground about 30 yards off; stood up facing us, flapping his wings and then stayed with his wings widespread and flat along the ground." This was while I was sketching the nest of four eggs, among sedge and under a bit of a bramble thicket.

The short-eared owl is always to the fore when plagues of voles occur, such as those in the Scottish Border counties in 1875-1876 and 1891-1892. Peter Adair, writing in the *Annals of Scottish Natural History* in 1892, recorded at least 301 nests of the short-eared owl in the areas of Teviot, Ettrick, Yarrow, Eskdalemuir and Moffat. These are only the nests found, and during the vole plagues the owls were rearing two broods in a season. On one farm of 3500 acres there were 40 nests. Large numbers of rough-legged buzzards came into the areas as well in the 1875 outbreak, obviously immigrants from Scandinavia where there was also a great increase in voles. Foxes also increased but did not confine their attention to voles, for one shepherd in Teviotdale opened a fox's earth in which he found—among many other birds—76 short-eared owls! As the plague declined, many owls starved, though a proportion doubtless emigrated from the region. Conversely, we may wonder how the immigrant birds become aware of the food supply which is suddenly prodigal in a district far from their original home!

## II.  SNIPE AND WOODCOCK

The drumming of the snipe (*Capella gallinago gallinago* L.) is one of the most delightful sounds of a calm spring evening. The snipe is much more a bird of the night than most waders, though at times they will drum extensively in full daylight. Two notes from my diary read :—

"*July* 17, 1922. Sandy Island, Orkney. We spent the day at Tafts Ness at the north end of the island where there were many snipe, some of them drumming. I could plainly see through my glasses the outside tail feathers on each side widely separated from the rest of the tail during this display, and during the downward swoop the wings are rapidly beating the whole time."

"*July* 19. To the north end again with Willie Peace. Many snipe about, drumming in all directions. Many start drumming almost directly after being flushed by us."

The word " drumming " is inappropriate. The word " bleating " much more readily conveys the real likeness of the sound, as it is exactly like the bleating of a goat. This sound is only and always produced during the rapid downward swoop of the bird and is caused by the rapid vibration of air through the two outside widely-spread tail feathers. There has been controversy as to whether the sound is vocal or instrumental, but by this time few people adhere to the vocal theory. Snipe usually drum in spring and early summer as part of their nuptial display, .but the sound can be heard occasionally as early as January and as late as September.

In the winter time the number of snipe in the British Isles is largely augmented by the arrival of others bred in more northern countries. But snipe are numerous residents here. The form breeding in Orkney and Shetland is the one common to the Faroes (*Capella gallinago faeroeensis* Brehm). Snipe are vagrant in their habits ; one day a locality may be full of snipe and next day they may all be gone. Also, some days they may be found singly, scattered about a wide expanse, and on others they will be collected in " wisps " of varying numbers. Snipe lie closer when they are single than in wisps, and in the morning than in the evening. At the latter time they are getting hungry and more restless, ready to move to their nightly feeding places.

When flushed, snipe take rapidly to the air and after careering about for some time fly right away. But sometimes, after this preliminary high flight, they will return and pitch near to where they were flushed. Where snipe are given sanctuary and never shot, they will often come to earth again fifty to a hundred yards from where they have been disturbed. Jack snipe are apt to do this as a normal type of behaviour.

It is curious to see a snipe perching on a post or railings after the fashion of a common sandpiper. They will do this occasionally in spring and may then be heard giving their " chipping " note, which is so different from the " scape " they utter when flushed.

The so-called " pin feathers " to be found on the outside edge— one on each wing—of snipe and woodcock, and which are reputed to have been used in days gone by by painters of miniatures, are referred to in Witherby's *Handbook* as being primary feathers, in which case these birds of this Order, and some of other Orders as well, possess eleven primaries and only nine primary coverts, instead of sets of ten and ten. I am inclined to think they are the outside feathers of the primary coverts, especially as this little thin, stiff feather appears to be laid on the upper surface of the primaries, as do the other primary coverts, and giving a wrong overlap if they are primaries. It is not easy to make this out quite satisfactorily from dried skins. It requires expert dissection of a bird in the flesh.*

I have looked through some of my skins haphazardly and find this feather in other Orders of birds, such as hawks (peregrine, merlin, kestrel, sparrow-hawk), ducks (teal, shoveler), wood-pigeon, owls (tawny, short-eared) and pheasant. It is not notice-able except on a very small scale in grouse and partridge. All the wading birds appear to have it.

Snipe and woodcock are notable for the fact of having the ear placed in a different position from that of other birds : it is placed underneath and almost in front of the eye instead of being consider-ably behind the eye.

There have always been controversies about the plumage characteristics and the habits of woodcock. It used to be thought that the sexes could be determined by the difference of the colour of the plumage, the smaller red-coloured birds being cocks and the larger, greyer birds hens. The amount of markings on the outer web of the outside primary feather was also thought to indicate whether a bird was of the year or fully adult. These views have been proved to be erroneous. Witherby's *Handbook* points out that proof from ringed nestlings in Ireland, Scotland, England and Sweden, subsequently shot in winter at all ages, shows such differences to be purely individual and not depending on age, sex or locality.

Few birds, surely, vary in weight so much as woodcock. I have weighed, and seen weighed, a good many birds, scaling from 8 to 15 oz. They are mostly between 10 and 13 oz., and the average of 336 woodcock is $11\frac{1}{2}$ oz.

They would appear to keep up their condition at times in spite of hard frosts. On one occasion in Norfolk, when skating was in full swing, I was shooting cock pheasants at the end of the season, and during that time we got sixteen woodcock, weighing 12, $11\frac{3}{4}$, $11\frac{1}{2}$, 11, $10\frac{1}{2}$, 11, 10, $10\frac{1}{2}$, $11\frac{1}{2}$, $11\frac{1}{2}$, 11, 9, 12, $11\frac{1}{2}$, 11, $10\frac{1}{2}$ oz. A thaw set in during the last two days of my visit, and though we shot some favourite woods there were no woodcock.

In England woodcock usually spend their daytime rest in woods, but are found at times in open country or in turnip fields,

---

* Since writing the above, I sent a wing of a freshly shot curlew to Dr Percy R. Lowe, who very kindly made an anatomical preparation of the wing, exposing the source of growth of the " pin " feather which, in a curlew, is very long and well developed. Dr Lowe sums up as follows : " Curlew, upper surface, 10 primaries, 10 upper major coverts (unreversed) lying to outer side of primaries, pin feather (unreversed) a covert of the 10th (outer) primary." This appears to corroborate what I have ventured to suggest on the subject.

when they are an easy shot, for they fly straight. Woodcock flushed in a wood fly zigzag perforce, in order to clear twigs and trees, and not to confound the man with the gun.

It is now a well-established fact that woodcock will sometimes carry their young, the act having been witnessed by several competent observers. I have never seen it happen myself, though once at Glencalvie, Ross-shire, in 1922, I saw a woodcock fly away from three young ones in a peculiar way. We flushed the bird from heather and birches at the side of the Carron where we were salmon fishing. I made some sketches of the young ones, whose wing feathers were just showing through the down, and of the appearance of the old bird as she flew away. The flight was so curious that I lay in ambush hoping to see it again. In this I was fortunate and had a much better view than the first time. She flew heavily and slowly with tail hanging and half spread; head and feet were also drooping. I could plainly see against the sky the feet with separated toes hanging below the tail. She flew for thirty yards and alighted on some stones at the foot of the river bank. There she flapped her wings for half a minute or so and appeared to become her normal self, running among the stones by the water and probing with her bill as if feeding. The keeper at Glencalvie told me he once shot a woodcock in mistake for a hawk. When he picked it up he found a young one with it, also dead, killed by the shot. Some years ago Lord William Percy told me he had noticed the same kind of flight in woodcock flushed from their young, and he thought the depressed tail might lead people to think a young bird was being carried. A sketch I made of this subject was published in *The Illustrated London News* of 14th April 1923.

When in very imminent danger a woodcock will spread wide its tail and switch it up over its back, thus displaying the glittering white tips of the under surface of the tail feathers (the upper surface of the tips of these feathers being smoky grey) in strong contrast to the black of the main part of the tail plumage. I have seen wounded birds do this when being picked up, and one displayed in like manner to a tiercel each time he approached it after knocking the woodcock down. Doubtless it is intimidatory display, but it is to be wondered how often it succeeds.

Woodcock make a considerable noise of wings when first flushed, sometimes almost as much as a hen pheasant; then the flight is quite noiseless and I have never heard them utter a note in the way that a snipe does. Their only cry seems to be that heard when the bird is " roding " in spring; it consists of alternate croaks and squeaks as the bird flits about silently on the course of its selected flying territory.

A WISP OF SNIPE

A woodcock really flies very fast, and one appreciates this while standing in rides of woods waiting for pheasants to come over. A woodcock will suddenly appear, flying low, quite silently and very fast, and is past and getting away among the tops of the " slop " almost before his presence is realised. Even if seen in front in time, a shot is often not possible on account of the lowness of its flight and the beaters coming up. As a rule he does not make a long flight before pitching again, but one can never tell, as he may turn off at a right angle from the direction he was last seen flying.

They are solitary birds and though a couple may be flushed sometimes, near enough to afford the possibility of a right and left, this proximity is only accidental. Sometimes a woodcock flushed by beaters will pitch in front of the guns. The first woodcock I ever shot came to grief in this way. I was a small youth at the time and was having the joy of being allowed to be an onlooker in a 300-acre cover shoot. I was allowed to have the keeper's gun for a few shots. This was a single-barrelled muzzle loader, which was duly loaded for me after each shot when rabbits were so polite as to come and sit in front of me. A woodcock came at one beat and pitched in front of me. I let fly immediately and it lay dead. It was the only woodcock of the day and was given to me as a token of my prowess. I duly stuffed that woodcock, very badly of course, but it gave me pleasure until such time as I was able to replace it with a better. Woodcocks are horrible birds to skin. They are always fat and their skins are so thin and tender that it is difficult to remove the fat without tearing the skin to pieces, especially the fat which lies along the feather tracts where it clings; and even if the skin is not torn it is hard to avoid pulling the feathers through the skin while scraping away the fat at their roots.

There is an old tale that woodcock will bind up an injury they may receive, using mud and grass. Possibly a bird with a broken leg would by chance gather a certain amount of rubbish about its leg which would mat and give the impression of a splinted and bandaged limb. Once such an event got into print it would be copied from book to book, regardless of the obvious absurdity of crediting the avian mind with such reasoning power.

Some people also believe that game birds have the power to suppress at will their body scent in order to baffle a hunting enemy. This is claimed to be proved by the fact of good dogs having been seen to fail to find game that was known to be very close and which had been flushed later when the dogs had given it up. But this proves nothing. Surely birds would always use such a natural gift and make retrievers useless. It is well known that at a certain stage of incubation, *i.e.* within a day or two of hatching, the scent is much stronger than at other times.

The ringing of nestling birds is proving of great value in adding to our knowledge of the movement of birds. Reference to Witherby's *Handbook* shows us that British-bred woodcock mostly stay within our shores, Scottish and northern English birds going to Ireland and the south of England, and some of those bred in the southern counties appear to cross to France, Spain and Portugal.

Our home stock is largely augmented in the winter months by migrants from northern Europe. Presumably none of these birds stay to nest but return to where they were bred.

I have seen several snipe and woodcock killed by trained peregrines which were waiting on. Once I saw a snipe taken by hand when a peregrine was waiting on for grouse. When lark hawking with merlins in Cornwall, I was told that snipe are taken by short-eared owls. If this is so, the owls must spot and take them on the ground, as they could never catch them on the wing.

One day when hawking we marked down a jack snipe on open grass, several yards from a freshwater ditch on a marsh, and when the tiercel had made his pitch we proceeded to walk up the snipe which was only sixty yards ahead. But we never found that jack snipe, although we groped about on our hands and knees in our efforts not to disappoint the hawk. In the same way, when lark hawking, I have frequently marked a lark that has put in, marked it carefully to within a few inches, and then failed to flush it again in spite of crawling about the grass for quite a long time. I suppose that on pitching, the quarry, whether snipe or lark, at once creeps away through the grass and thus makes its escape.

One final note : snipe's eggs are very large for the size of the bird. An average weight for a snipe is 4 oz., and that of a hen partridge about 14 oz., yet a snipe's egg appears to be larger than a partridge's, though I have never weighed them.

### III. The Bearded Tit

Of all our passerine birds the species that are most restricted in their locality in Britain are the crested tit and the bearded tit, the former being confined to parts of the Highlands and the latter to Norfolk and Suffolk. Several other very local species such as the cirl bunting, woodlark, marsh warbler and Dartford warbler are yet of much wider distribution.

The bearded tit (*Panurus biarmicus biarmicus* L.) is not a true tit but is separated in a genus by itself. It is entirely an

DUCKS RISING

inhabitant of dense reed beds and sedge, where its presence may be detected by hearing its sweet note, a soft and musical " ting ting " several times repeated.

The bird conceals its nest low down among the lower tangle of reeds, the nest being made externally of shreds of dead reeds and lined with the old flower heads of the reeds and an occasional feather. The eggs are unlike those of the true tits, being marked sparingly with scratchy streaks instead of the characteristic spots. Moreover, the clutch is much smaller in number of eggs ; five to seven is the usual number, though occasionally eight to twelve have been found.

Like most birds, the bearded tit has to cope with many enemies. One of these is its rare neighbour of the marsh, the bittern (*Botaurus stellaris stellaris* L.). It is well known that young bitterns when disturbed in the nest will disgorge their last meal. I have seen this happen—the meal on that occasion being of young eels—but I have been told by an eye-witness of young bearded tits being disgorged. No one would suggest that bearded tits' nests are sought particularly, but like other members of the Family Ardeidæ which normally feed on fish, the bittern is not averse from young birds it can swallow whole.

An old bittern stalking among the reeds so silently and un-obtrusively has many chances of finding nests of bearded tits, reed buntings, yellow wagtails and water rails, and for this reason is somewhat of a menace to a bird sanctuary unless his numbers are controlled.

The bearded tit is a very tame bird. A flock will keep company with the Norfolk reed cutters as they follow their work and the birds know themselves to be safe. Hard winters on the Broads greatly cut down the numbers of the bearded tit, though it seems to be a species with good recuperative powers.

## IV.  THE CRESTED TIT

Although the crested tit (*Parus cristatus scoticus* Prazak) is just as local in Scotland as the bearded tit is in England, it is nevertheless spread over a larger area of country. The old wild pine forests of the Spey Valley, particularly about Rothiemurchus and Abernethy, appear to provide the necessary environment for food and nesting. Solid stands of coniferous timber do not attract the bird. Indeed, some of these close plantations are almost empty country for birds of any kind except roosting wood-pigeons.

It is rather to be wondered why this species has hitherto been so local, and why it has not spread to many other parts of the

Highlands where there are open pine woods which seem to our eyes a good enough habitat for the crested tit. As a matter of fact a pair has been seen in May in such a place on the north-west Highland coast. The pines were about ninety years old and there were considerable stretches of open country between the clumps dotted with occasional trees. No nest was found and they were not seen in the following year.

One feature of the Spey Valley forests is the presence of so many juniper bushes, the berries of which are eaten by the crested tit in addition to the seeds of ripe pine cones and insects and larvæ. Another is that in these old forests there is a sufficiency of decaying timber and old stumps to afford nesting sites for these little birds.

It would be a good thing if the crested tit could establish itself in some such district remote from the Spey region and not be seen for a few years, because in its home range the nesting localities are well known and consistently harried by egg collectors. Perhaps this is the main reason why they have not spread much beyond this bit of original forest.

Egg collecting is a ticklish subject. There is reason to doubt whether moderate collecting for scientific purposes is harmful, for such depradation must represent a very small fraction of the total natural and inevitable loss of eggs in the nest. The trouble lies with people who style themselves oologists and who collect as many whole clutches as they can. The rarer the bird becomes, the keener are these men to take British clutches, and they will resort to remarkable subterfuges to get them. It is surely a mean thing to employ labourers and gamekeepers to run the gauntlet of stealing clutches of eggs of carefully protected birds.

The extremists of protection are apt to do harm, for overstating a good cause tends to drive the moderates into the opposite camp. What our propaganda should aim at is a changed attitude of mind, which would limit egg-collecting more surely than prohibitions.

Cruelty is a word to be used with caution in connection with egg-collecting, for the bird's mind is so far removed in type from ours. The bird follows a chain of reactions, and if this is broken, as is possible in countless accidental ways, the bird seems unable to carry on from that point, but either gives up completely or goes back to the very beginning again. A break in the weather will cause a bird to desert eggs or young, as Eliot Howard has shown, or the migratory urge may overtake birds rearing a late brood and cause them to leave the young. However, let these remarks not overlay the fact obvious to anyone that the removal of a clutch of eggs causes suffering of some kind to the parent birds.

CROSSBILLS, WITH NEST AND EGGS
Fairburn, Ross-shire.  Feb. 20, 1907.

## V. THE CROSSBILL

Ross-shire is the headquarters of the crossbill in Britain. Spasmodically it is resident in many places throughout the country —as far south as Bournemouth and common in Ireland in places. It is not necessary here to go into details of the difference between the common crossbill (*Loxia curvirostra curvirostra* L.) and the Scottish crossbill (*Loxia curvirostra scotica* Hart), as these can be found in Witherby's *Handbook of British Birds*. Suffice it to say that the chief difference appears to be in the rather more massive beak of the Scottish bird, which approximates to that of the parrot-crossbill (*Loxia pityopsittacus* Borkh.), which species has been recorded only as a rare vagrant in the British Isles.

Crossbills are very sociable in their habits, and during the time they are not nesting may be seen in flocks of varying numbers, feeding on the cones of various fir trees. If another flock passes anywhere near them while so occupied, the stationary flock will call loudly to them, and the invitation is generally accepted.

In dull or windy weather they are often restless, flying to and fro and perching for no longer than a few moments, and all the while uttering their call-note, which is not unlike that of the greater spotted woodpecker but not quite so loud and sharp.

Sometimes they are so silent while feeding that their presence would go unnoticed but for the falling of cones as each bird finishes extracting the seeds. They often use their bills parrot fashion as they make their way along the branches to get at the fir cones. These they dexterously cut off and carry in their beak until they reach a suitable perch, when the cone is transferred to one foot and the seeds are extracted by the tongue, the beak being used in characteristic fashion to prize open the cone.

They nest very early in the year, as the following notes from my diary testify :

"*February* 20, 1907. Fairburn, Ross-shire. With Stirling to make studies of crossbills and nests for a couple of pictures he wants me to paint for him. His keepers knew of five nests so we spent the afternoon among the birds. One of these nests was practically inaccessible, right at the top of a Scots fir, on an out-lying branch, so we left it alone. Another was found only to-day and had two eggs. This was in a small Scots fir about 25 feet up and built against the main stem, which appears to be an unusual position. Another was at the top of a high fir and contained one egg a few days before. Now, there were only broken egg-shells, so I kept this nest.

" I went up to the other two nests which were both high in

fairly tall Scots firs. The first was deserted and had only two eggs. I sat in the tree and made a sketch of the nest and its surroundings. It was snowing fast all the time. I took the eggs and then one of the men came up with a saw and cut off the branch with the nest for me to take away.

"The next nest I visited contained three eggs much incubated. A lot of snow now and curling on the ponds."

"*February* 23. Went to the crossbill's nest in which we left two eggs on 20th. The nest was deserted, full of snow and the eggs cracked with the frost."

"*February* 24. We noticed a pair of crossbills fly past once or twice, and back again in the same direction. So we laid in wait along their line of flight and soon marked them down to their nest which the hen was building at the end of a horizontal branch of a Scots fir about 30 feet from the ground. The cock bird took no part in the building preparations, but sat still at the top of the tree. He accompanied the hen each time she went off for more building material, which journeys seemed always to be in the same direction."

"*February* 25. The hen crossbill still busy with her building."

Although crossbills feed mostly on fir cones, they will also eat other kinds of seeds, and insects at times.

"*June* 12, 1919. Woodhall Spa, Lincolnshire. While butterfly hunting in Bracken Wood to-day I saw a flock of crossbills. They were at the top of some oak trees (of which this wood is mostly composed) which are almost denuded of their leaves by countless hosts of caterpillars. The birds appeared to be feeding on the caterpillars, as they were incessantly picking them off the twigs and leaves; but my glasses failed actually to discover anything in their beaks. At least one of them was a beautiful red bird. They may have bred here as there are plenty of coniferous trees."

I had never heard of them breeding in that district and this was the only time I ever saw them in Lincolnshire.

Crossbills are very thirsty birds. I have seen one in my garden take as many as seventeen sips in succession. And they are so fearless that I have seen one come down to drink when I was only four yards away from him, standing on the open lawn.

There is another note in my diary on the same point:

"*April* 26, 1931. Camberley. A crossbill with two fledged young ones in the garden. One of the young flew down to the guttering at the edge of the roof of the verandah of my studio. The old one, a dull red male, came down to it but was a bit nervous as I was standing only a few feet away. It flew into a fir tree near at hand, but soon came down again and fed the young one by regurgitation without minding my presence."

When I was in Ireland some years ago, I was told the inhabitants of that district (Co. Down) sometimes catch crossbills with nooses on the end of fishing rods, and from what one has seen of their tameness this can well be believed.

When kept in captivity, as I have experienced, the cock birds never keep their beautiful red plumage, but when they moult come into the green plumage. Although these birds are extremely good-tempered with others of their own kind, they much object to other species of birds being in the same cage with them, and relentlessly hunt them about all day. Also, they are destructive to any wood-work of which the cage may be composed. Perhaps these remarks are superfluous nowadays, as it is illegal to keep wild-caught birds in cages.

## VI. WOODPECKERS

The most common of the three resident species of woodpecker in Britain is certainly the green woodpecker (*Picus viridis pluvius* Hart.). All the woodpeckers are far more plentiful in England than they are in Scotland, where they are rare birds—and they are rarer still in Ireland. The great spotted woodpecker (*Dryobates major anglicus* Hart.) is the only species breeding in Scotland, through which country it has greatly extended its range since 1887, when it was thought to be extinct in Scotland. It is even to be found in one or two wooded glens in the North-West Highlands.

The great black woodpecker (*Picus martius* L.) has on several occasions been reported to have been observed in England, but so far has not been admitted to the British List, the evidence being insufficient. There have also been known escapes from captivity. This bird would be a great acquisition to the British avi-fauna, especially in those parts of dense pine woods, for it is essentially a bird of such forests in northern Europe.

It is considerably larger than the green woodpecker and is sooty black in the whole of its plumage except the crown of the head, which is crimson in the male; in the female this colour is confined to the back of the head. The eye is cream coloured and the pupil appears to be not circular but smudged into the iris towards the beak, or perhaps the pupil is circular, but the iris has a smudge of black against the pupil. This I noticed in a fine example of the bird in the Zoo on 3rd April 1898. The beak is whitish yellow in the basal half.

My personal experiences of this bird have been in Sweden, and though I have heard the note of the bird in Norway, I have not actually seen it there. It is shy, and living in the dense pine woods it is much more often heard than seen. It has two character-istic notes which, once heard, are never to be forgotten. When taking wing or being disturbed it utters a grating, crackling cry, and on settling again it gives forth a very loud, clear, mellow whistle. This whistle note can be heard a long way off and is very sweet when heard coming from the pine woods a mile away across the ice-bound lakes in winter.

Being shy and not numerous, it took me a whole winter and spring to collect two specimens, a cock and a hen. The first one I followed for a long time among the fir trees, and at last got close enough to shoot him as he was hammering at a stump among a dense thicket of young growth of firs.

This was in the autumn of 1881 and the bird was solitary. The hen bird was shot in the following spring, on 28th March, and it was in the company of its mate. I stalked them in a small wood of scattered birch, but was unable to get a shot at the cock. Going again to the same place at the same time the next day, in hopes of the cock bird being there, I was disappointed, for he had left the neighbourhood.

On 6th May 1882 I was told of a black woodpecker's nest in a hole in a birch tree. There were two eggs.

The green woodpecker has the longest tongue of all the European species that I have seen, even longer than that of the black wood-pecker. Green woodpeckers take a great deal of food from the ground and are frequently seen on lawns and in gardens, foraging for insect life, especially ants. But they can play havoc with the turf, for they dig considerable holes as they ply their powerful beaks. One forgives them a lot for their ornamental quality.

The great spotted woodpecker appears to have a more varied diet than the other British species, for besides insects it will eat seeds from cones. I have watched one on a nearly vertical branch of a tree with the fir cone held in one foot while it hammered with its beak to force apart the plates and reach the seeds at their base. When discarded, the cone has the same appearance as one dealt with by a crossbill, the plates not being broken off but forced apart so that they are sticking outwards.

Squirrels, on the other hand, when eating the contents of a fir cone, bite the plates off altogether, so that when discarded there is nothing left except the core of the cone. The ground below the tree is littered with bitten-off plates.

The great spotted woodpecker will, moreover, come to bird tables in winter time and will eat beef fat with the utmost relish. It frequents coniferous woods more than the other British species, but may nevertheless be found in wholly deciduous woods.

I have never seen the lesser spotted woodpecker (*Dryobates minor comminutus* Hart.) in other than deciduous-wooded country. This little bird is the least shy of them all and can be approached at times (when it is not at the top of a high elm tree) to within a few yards.

Both the great and lesser spotted woodpeckers perform the drumming operation, but the green woodpecker does not do so. This sound is mostly to be heard in the springtime when its use may have significance in advertising ownership of territory. The earliest I have ever heard it is 24th January 1934, when I watched a lesser spotted woodpecker drumming on the branch of an acacia tree in the garden of Thelveton Hall, Norfolk; and I have seen a great spotted woodpecker drumming in August in Wiltshire.

This drumming is unquestionably instrumental and not vocal. The fact of its having been seen performed on corrugated iron, producing quite a different sound from that on wood, is surely sufficient evidence. The extremely rapid motion of the head during drumming can be seen if one is close enough. The note in my diary concerning the lesser spotted woodpecker mentioned above says: " Could distinctly see through my glasses the movement of the head."

Another note on this subject :

" *May* 3, 1903. Singapore. Before leaving here at 9.0 a.m. took a short stroll on shore. A small woodpecker was on a dead stump about 12 feet from the ground . . . it kept drumming just below what looked like its nest hole. While drumming its whole body was vibrated right down to the end of its tail. . . . It flew away when I approached to within a few yards of it. But on my return a few minutes later I found it back again and drumming at intervals."

One of the arguments used by those who assert that the noise is vocal is the fact that when the wood is inspected no marks of the bill are found. But the rapid tapping on hard wood may be quite sufficient to produce the sound and yet not mark it. It is a very different action from the powerful digging when obtaining food or making nest holes. Leading ornithologists at the present day (1944) are almost unanimous in the view that the drumming of the woodpecker is mechanical. So long ago as 1919 Dr Julian Huxley gave it as his considered opinion that the drumming is made mechanically, not vocally, and expressed the view that it was without doubt of sexual significance. Mr N. D. Pullen, in a recent number of *British Birds* (vol. 37), gave an interesting account of experiments made with a microphone, from which definite evidence was obtained, other than visual, that the bird's bill makes actual contact with the surface. Huxley's opinion that the drumming has some sexual significance—putting a stimulant to the other member of the pair—is supported by a field note by Dr Percy Lowe, who writes to me as follows: " In the Grand Cayman Island I was standing under a tree in the early morning when one of its beautiful woodpeckers began drumming on the main trunk low down. It was obvious to anyone that it was doing it by tapping with its bill, and also the reason for it, for presently the female flew across the valley and joined it."

I have twice found a ring of feathers of the great spotted woodpecker indicating that the bird had been the victim of a hawk, probably a sparrow-hawk.

GREAT SKUA, WITH NEST AND EGGS
Mid Yell, Shetlands. June 23, 1914.

# PART III

## SOME SHETLAND MEMORIES

### I. The Great Skua

When the late E. G. B. Meade-Waldo and the late W. R. Ogilvie-Grant and I were in Shetland in 1914 we visited Hermaness, the north-west corner of Unst, the northernmost island of the British Isles. Hermaness is a high headland overlooking the rocks of Muckle Flugga where the lighthouse is. It is a truly thrilling place, for not only are the sea cliffs full of birds of the auk tribe, kittiwakes and shags, with Atlantic grey seals in the breakers at the foot, but on the short heather and grasses of the plateau is the headquarters of the great skua (*Stercorarius skua skua* Brünn) in the British Isles.

When we were there, the watcher, Edwardson, told us there were 73 pairs of " bonxies," as the Shetlanders call them, breeding on Hermaness that year. Twenty-three years before that time the stock was down to three pairs, and the few pairs on the other Shetland breeding station of Foula were also in jeopardy. Mr Thomas Edmonston first paid a watcher in May 1891 and it is to him, and to Mr Scott of Melby who owned Foula, that we have this magnificent bird still as a breeding species. Now, in the 1940's, the great skua breeds also on Saxavord, Unst ; Yell, Noss, North Mainland, Fetlar, Hascosay, Bressay, Mousa, Fair Isle, and on Hoy, Orkney. This is a fine example of what protection can do.

Besides the bonxies, my friends and I saw a much larger number of " scooties," Arctic or Richardson's skua (*Stercocarius parasiticus* L.). They are much more numerous in Shetland generally and with their active flight and loud cries are very much in evidence.

But even in 1914 the Great Skua was spreading quickly. We saw four pairs on Mid-Yell, ten or twelve pairs on Hascosay, and a few pairs on Fetlar. Meade-Waldo and I were there again in 1922 and found twelve pairs of Great Skuas on Noss, and three pairs on North Roe. James Hay, the watcher there, told us that many of the red-throated divers' eggs had been destroyed. He thought bonxies were chiefly responsible ; but was not sure, and in one case at any rate blamed ravens, for he saw a raven with grown young close to a recently destroyed nest. This, of course, was not convincing proof. Hay had also seen a scootie in the act of taking divers' eggs. Probably all these scavenging sort of birds —ravens, hooded crows, black-backed gulls, bonxies and scooties— are responsible for a certain amount of egg-stealing and divers' eggs have no natural protection.

The Great Skuas give their nest away by incessant stooping at the intruder if he approaches too close to the nest, but do not go through the so-called injury-feigning antics as do the scooties under similar circumstances. They rarely hit you as they make their long slanting swoop, but just lift and glide over one's head, coming so close that it seems easy to catch the bird were one to suddenly raise a hand. But if this is tried it will be found quite unsuccessful. I have been hit by both bonxie and scootie—and such a whack by the latter that I thought my companion had thrown a clod of earth at me.

The nests of the Great Skua seem to be invariably lined with light reddish dead grass, which makes them rather conspicuous in the dark peaty surroundings. The nests themselves are quite shallow depressions, not banked up with moss as gulls' nests are; and the eggs seem always to be placed a little apart from each other, never quite touching. There are only two eggs to a clutch.

The young ones very soon leave the nest and are found sheltering anywhere, under peat-hags, in tufts of grass and irregularities of the ground; the two are never together but anything up to twenty yards apart. We found one lying quite comfortably half submerged in a shallow pool. Another had a large mackerel lying alongside it. When first hatched they are sooty in colour, nearly as dark as young scooties, but quickly pass through dusky cinnamon to a greyish fawn colour.

A lucky find was registered on our first visit to Hermaness:

"*June* 20, 1914. Found a dead bonxie, perfectly fresh and in beautiful plumage. We found that it had swallowed a large fish hook with a stout piece of cord attached to it. The hook was fast down the gullet and the cord protruded some way from the mouth. I made a good skin of this, the bird on dissection proving to be a male. We found another dead one, but it was ancient. Ogilvie-Grant took it for the skeleton." He was at that time Keeper of the Ornithological Department of the British Museum (Natural History).

The smaller skuas are very fast fliers. It is extraordinary to watch how soon they can overhaul any unfortunate gull or tern they may espy having caught a fish or anything else from the sea.

GREAT BLACK-BACKED GULL, WITH NEST AND EGGS
North Roe, Shetlands. June 30, 1914.

The skua very soon forces its victim to give up the prey and takes it himself. Probably no peregrine would ever have a chance of catching one of these birds.

I saw a couple of scooties on Hascosay twice in succession knock down to the ground a lesser black-backed gull, but it was impossible to be sure whether they actually hit the gull or whether the latter simply fell from them to avoid the attack.

## II. SOME BRITISH GULLS

The largest and grandest-looking of the six species of gull breeding in these Islands is the great black-backed gull (*Larus marinus* L.). Little in the way of food comes amiss to this omnivorous bird—fish, carrion, living birds and garbage. I understand that on the great seal nursery of North Rona, this gull efficiently scavenges the afterbirths and the carcasses of dead seal calves. The big black-back is a terror to puffins and to any bird it can tackle, and it has the name of being troublesome when lambs are newly born (convincing evidence is hard to come by), yet Fraser Darling says that in the two seasons he spent at the seal nurseries of the Treshnish Isles and North Rona, he never saw evidence of a black-back attacking a live seal calf.

In most places this gull nests solitarily or on the outskirts of a colony of herring gulls (*Larus argentatus argentatus* Pontopp.) or lesser black-backed gulls (*Larus fuscus graelsii* Brehm). All these three species nest on the flat in Shetland, as distinct from the kittiwake (*Rissa tridactyla tridactyla* L.) which is purely a cliff-nesting species. It is probable, however, that the great black-back naturally tends to be gregarious, but that restricted numbers prevent such a habit in many places. The species has increased in recent years and definite colonies are arising. For example, there is the old-established colony on the top of the Holm of Noss, a stack of solid rock rising 160 feet from the sea, its top being covered with rank herbage of campion, sorrel, seapink and grass. We counted nearly two hundred pairs in 1914 and there seemed more when we were there again in 1922. The biggest colony in the British Isles is certainly that on North Rona, where Fraser Darling in *A Naturalist on Rona* says there are well over five hundred pairs. The same observer has also recorded an old-established colony of about a hundred pairs on the outermost islet of the Summer Isles, Glas Leac Beag. All these considerable colonies are on rocks or islands difficult of access by human beings.

We were told there used to be a bridge between the Holm and Noss and that a few sheep were grazed there. We were also told that since the bridge was non-existent, a venturesome man tried to get to the top, starting by way of the mast of a boat. He succeeded, but came to grief on the way down and was killed.

The bird life of the Shetlands in May and June is breath-taking in its wonder of variety and numbers. Here are some bare notes from my diary of 1922 :

"*June* 29, 1922. Noss. Many lesser black-backed gulls in various colonies on the ground, some with eggs, others hatched. Saw one very handsome bright green clutch of three. Six ravens on the Noup and 16 gannets there. Many fulmars and thousands of guillemots ; also many puffins, razorbills, kittiwakes and herring gulls. The sea below was thick with birds. We could see only one guillemot's egg through our glasses. We saw no whimbrel, but Jamieson reports that two pairs bred and that the young got off all right. Plenty of eiders, eggs from 2 to 5, and saw two broods of young ones, 3 and 4. Found two eiders' eggs which had been eaten. A small colony of common gulls (*Larus canus canus* L.) on the grass. Three eggs in one nest, also young ones elsewhere, a few days old. About 12 pairs of bonxies and many scooties ; found five nests of the latter, three with eggs, one with one young one about two days old, and the other with a young one just out and a dark green egg. One bonxie very handsome type, light fawn colour on whole of neck and underparts, with dark cap and face, very conspicuous standing alongside a normal bird."

I found the remains of many kittiwakes at one place on Bressay, which looked very much as if it were a peregrine's feeding place. It was near a freshwater loch where the kittiwakes were in the habit of coming in from the sea to bathe in the fresh water. Such a habit of freshwater bathing cannot be commonly indulged by the kittiwake for it is essentially an oceanic gull. I have known this species remain with a ship the whole way across the Atlantic, though of course I could not swear they were the same birds. I once found a kittiwake in a hedge at Sawbridgeworth, Essex, probably blown inland by a gale.

In the north of Norway most of the gulls seen are kittiwakes, sometimes in vast numbers which seem to collect in a very short time. Little patches of small fish jumping about in the waters of the fjord will immediately attract all the gulls in the district. I remember one night seeing four boats fishing a mile offshore near Honingsvaag, and the flock of gulls about them was so dense as to completely mask the boats from time to time. A good many Arctic skuas were in attendance as usual.

It is remarkable how clean and spotless in plumage gulls can keep themselves, considering their feeding habits. Even in London,

HERRING GULLS
On the Sussex Coast.

the gulls (and the pelicans) of the parks seem to keep themselves free of grime. The black-headed gull (*Larus ridibundus ridibundus* L.) is the most common in London, though his head is almost white during autumn and winter. I might add as a note of interest that I well remember the gulls' first appearance as a London bird in the severe winter of 1880-1881. Finding themselves well treated, they returned each year thereafter and everyone knows how tame they are. Londoners were delighted with the gulls that winter, when lumps of ice floated down the Thames and the snow was so deep that hansoms were being driven tandem.

# PART IV

# MEMORIES OF GAME BIRDS

## I. THE RED GROUSE

The red grouse (*Lagopus scoticus scoticus* Lath.) has the distinction of being indigenous to the British Isles and nowhere else in the world. Its nearest ally is the Scandinavian willow grouse (*Lagopus lagopus*) or " dal rype," which is similar to our grouse in all respects except that during the whole year it has all the lower plumage below the breast, and the primary feathers and greater part of the rest of the wing, pure white. The willow grouse moults out in autumn to pure white except for the tail feathers which are always black. This is the bird which appears as ptarmigan in the poulterers' shops. The true ptarmigan (*Lagopus mutus millaisi* Hart.) is a much smaller bird and the summer plumage is much greyer and more finely vermiculated than that of the willow grouse. I should think the weight of willow grouse would compare closely with that of our species, but I regret to say I have never weighed either willow grouse or ptarmigan, although I have shot them in Norway.

The individual variation in the plumage of our grouse is very great. Some, with the exception of the neck, which always seems to retain the chestnut-coloured feathers, are almost black all over, with sparse red markings on the upper plumage and no white markings on the underparts. Others are more or less heavily spotted with white underneath, irrespective of whether the upper plumage is black, red or yellow in coloration. Hen birds are often as black as the cocks, and this dark plumage is attained at an early stage in life, in fact at their first moult in autumn. There can be considerable variation on the same moor.

The Irish grouse, recently granted subspecific rank as *Lagopus scoticus hibernicus* (Kleinschm.) is inclined to the red and yellow type of plumage. The grouse of the Outer Hebrides are now placed in this subspecies. Personally, I cannot distinguish the Welsh grouse from the Irish birds.

In the old days black plumage was thought to be a sign of disease, as sparsely feathered legs and feet were also. Of course, it is now well known that a grouse moults its leg and feet feathers in course of its ordinary moult, and early in the season every grouse

A GROUSE FAMILY

Both parents keep watch and ward over the chicks.

shot will be more or less in moult. Their feet feather up much later in the season.

I got a good many excellent specimens of the very dark and black types of grouse on Strathgartney when my old friend Hugh Mann had it over thirty years ago. He had over 30,000 acres, from the grounds of the Trossachs Hotel to very nearly the far end of Loch Katrine, the lodge, Brenachoil, being set back a little way up the slope from the north shore of the loch. There was plenty of wood, oak and birch along the loch-side and all the rest was grouse and deer ground. It went to over 2000 feet in parts and was good for fifteen to twenty stags and a good lot of grouse. There were always eagles, buzzards and ravens to be watched. There was an eagle's eyrie on the place, though I never saw it. Strathgartney had never been driven, but Hugh Mann got more keepers on to the place, put up rows of butts and more than doubled any previous bag that had been made there. On bye days the low ground afforded plenty of sport, there being rabbits in plenty, and driving the wooded parts would always produce a few blackcock, woodcock and pheasants.

There were some very sporting butts on the high ground, especially on Ben An, where one could get great variety of shots— high overhead, right down below as well as level ones. There was one butt which was quite the most difficult from which to shoot that I have ever known. It was the one on the left flank of that line of butts and had level ground in front of it, but was at the foot of a 60-foot vertical precipice. Set back from the top edge of this precipice was the next butt, called the Eagle's on account of its position. From their relative setting the shooting from either of these butts was perfectly safe, but it meant that the man in the lower one had to keep a look-out not only in front of him but high overhead to the right as well. This meant some mighty quick shooting for they were over one's head as soon as they were in sight at all; and birds shot from the Eagle would come rattling down about the lower butt.

Next to the Eagle was one we called the Gully butt, as it commanded a deep gully and was perched on the top of the right side. Here one of the guns came to grief one day. Jack Mann was leaning against the side when he and half the butt fell down the gully. Luckily he fell into deep heather without hitting any big stones, so that neither he nor his gun suffered any damage.

Grouse are fast fliers, but the speed of flight of different birds is deceptive; a blackcock, for example, making many less wing beats to the minute than a red grouse, will rapidly overhaul him. A grouse's flight consists of alternate periods of quickly moving its wings and then skimming with set wings, the head all the time being well raised. Seen on a level with one's eyes and going straight away, the whole head is well above the level of the back. After the skimming period the bird makes a sudden fall of about a foot before resuming the flapping part. This sudden fall can be most disconcerting when one is at the butts.

Grouse fly very silently, with none of the rattle characteristic of partridge. They are not vocal on the wing, except that the cock cries as he rises and just as he comes to earth again. This " go-back " note is given even when the bird puts in hard pressed by a peregrine. A grouse in full flight rocks his body from side to side, but when skimming keeps on an even keel. They generally fly fairly close to the ground, following its undulations and do not commonly alight until they are out of sight. This necessitates dogs for grouse hawking. English setters are most satisfactory for either hawking or shooting grouse because of their conspicuous colour.

Late in the season grouse pack in large numbers. So do partridges (*Perdix perdix perdix* L.) where there are enough of them ; I have seen several hundreds come over the guns in one pack in Norfolk. But there is this difference between a pack of grouse and of partridges coming over in a drive : the grouse coming from a much larger area of country will often be so much strung out in depth that the guns over which they come may get several minutes of shooting before the pack has passed. Partridges may be spread out laterally to give shots to the whole line of guns, but are over and gone within a few seconds. The noise of a pack of partridges rising from a field of roots may be likened to that of a squadron of cavalry galloping over the same ground.

I have weighed about 150 grouse and the heaviest was 29½ oz., shot in Kintyre on 26th September 1906. The next heaviest was 28 oz., shot at Cortachy on 19th August 1911. In weighing these birds the contents of the crop should be deducted, as I have taken as much as 2 oz. of heather from a grouse's crop. They have their chief feed late in the day, so grouse shot in the last drive of the day will be found to have their crops crammed, and these birds will therefore weigh more. A general average of weights of adult grouse would be 24-25 oz. for cocks and 20-22 oz. for hens.

Of the three methods of grouse shooting—driving, walking-up in line, and shooting over dogs—each has its advocates and it is largely a matter of individual choice. Driving is the most expensive and needs most organisation, both of men and strategy. Some people say driving does not give the guns enough exercise, but there are plenty of moors which give one quite enough scrambling about. What is more to be deplored is the good chance of getting very cold.

COCK AND HEN GROUSE, WHITE SPOTTED VARIETY

It is also possible to get eaten alive with midges, which seem to lurk in grouse butts. The Lord preserve you then if you are a non-smoker.

There is plenty to do when you get to the butts and before the birds come over. If the ground is broken you must make sure of the line of the butts, especially marking the position of the butts either side of you if they should happen to be out of sight. A good keeper will have made a cairn of stones or peats on the brow for your guidance. Then you critically examine the ground before you and mark the undulations and nature of it. If very stony you will know that at low grouse you must shoot only to your straight front. An oblique shot may cause a bad accident from ricochet pellets to an occupant of one of the other butts. You will see that the floor of the butt is level, clear of obstructions to allow free footwork, and you will adjust the height of the butt to suit your own shooting position; and, finally, you will stow your dog where he will be out of the way and comfortably fixed for himself.

Then you make up your mind where you think the grouse will first make their appearance, and being usually right, you will be ready for the first covey. If there is a good view of the ground in front it is interesting to watch the course of the drive; the grouse can be seen getting up a long way off, and getting bigger in your vision as they come nearer. Perhaps they will swerve out at a flank and you will see the concealed flankers spring up at the right moment, wave their flags, and turn the birds back into the drive. Grouse are more amenable to flanking than any other of our game birds.

Walking in line after grouse is splendid exercise, especially on a hilly moor on a hot day. A strict line should be kept, which is easy enough on ground where the whole line can be seen, but not in rough ground. It is a mistake to walk too fast. Sometimes there is a delightful interval of rest when there is a delay in the dogs finding a bird that has been shot and the weary fellow (myself) sits down thankfully in the heather, pulls out his pipe, and hopes it may be quite a while yet before the dog succeeds.

I well remember such a walk on 30th August 1928. Six guns set out from Struy, picked up with the keepers after an eight-mile walk uphill. From then until evening we went forward steadily in perfect weather and got 97 grouse. The night was spent in a permanent hut maintained for this beat, and next day we walked back again in line, bagging 104 grouse, one hare, and one adder.

Shooting over dogs has the added charm of seeing the dogs

I

work, and to lovers of pointers and setters this form of grouse shooting appeals more than the others. Fewer guns are required, not more than two or three for each beat, and the walking is not quite so strenuous as the dogs cover so much of the ground. The guns can move leisurely and even sit down sometimes while the dogs are working. It is grand to see the dogs quartering the ground at their swinging elastic gallop, and to watch them taking notice of their handler's whistle before going off again in the direction indicated. Then the sudden stop in the midst of the gallop as the first scent of grouse comes across their nostrils, and the cautious advance to find the grouse and ultimately the rigid point; while the guns advance, each a bit to one side of the dog, ready for the covey when it flushes. When the heather is in good bloom a trail of dusty pollen flies behind the track of the dog, like the dust behind a motor-car on a dry Highland road. The pollen is sometimes so profuse that it flies up into the eyes of the guns as they walk through the heather and causes discomfort. Plain glass spectacles are a great help on such occasions.

## II. Grouse, Partridges, Ptarmigan, Black Game and Capercaillie

In these days of advanced knowledge and exact science it is disconcerting to find how little has been proved absolutely with regard to the life histories of even our game birds, which have been the subject of much amateur study.

Sport is full of traditions and theories about them, some unproved and untrue but which are nevertheless firmly believed by many sportsmen and keepers who have observed game birds closely all their lives.

Take for example the well-known and generally believed idea of eliminating as many old cock birds as possible—and in some cases young cocks also—as a means of improving the stock. In theory this is splendid. Old cocks certainly harry the breeding pairs, and even if they do breed themselves, require a large territory and have smaller broods. But when is a partridge or a grouse an old cock? At what age does he cease to become useful at stud? And how do you tell an old cock from a young one once he has attained full plumage?

You can certainly tell the age of a partridge up to the age of eighteen months when in the hand, but once the second moult (in the autumn of the year after he is hatched) has been completed, how is anyone to say whether he is only a previous year's bird, and therefore good for breeding purposes, or a third or a fourteenth

A COVEY OF DRIVEN PARTRIDGES

season's bird ? And in the case of grouse who can possibly tell an old from a young bird even late in the season of being hatched, for the beak is then strong enough to resist the broken beak test which is good enough for early in the season ?

The only thing I can suggest is that in the young cock the comb over the eye is thinner and less brilliant than in older birds. The comb tends to become thicker and more ragged at the edges with age. But, of course, this is discernible only when the grouse is in hand.

It is more or less easy to pick out the cocks from a rising covey as they usually crow as they get up, but driven grouse are quite another matter. They are silent, and unless sunlight is on them from the direction they are facing when coming to the guns, they all look black against the sky.

One is always told that the habits of old cocks give them away, as these birds are supposed to congregate on the high ground late in the season. What absolute proof is there that they are all old ones ? Granted that cocks do congregate in this manner, why not mixed packs of old and young ?

Some moor owners advocate shooting cocks at all times in preference to hens, and sometimes go so far as to shoot only cocks during a day's walking-up or shooting over dogs, the theory being that if there is a preponderance of hens the cocks will tend to be polygamous. But has this been so thoroughly investigated as to be proved ? It is no proof to say that subsequent seasons with an improved stock justifies the theory, unless such a result is apparent over a long period of time and in several places. There are many other environmental factors which may come into play, and it takes careful analysis and research to find such factors, note them, and interpret their effects.

It is possible that a shortage of cocks would result in some hens leaving the moor when the breeding season came round. Now, does a cock grouse range about looking for a hen or does he take up a definite territory and by his crowing and becking display induce a hen to stay with him ? I believe the latter course to be the true one ; if I am right, a shortage of cocks would certainly mean a loss of hens to areas better supplied. Some game birds are naturally polygamous, but in the wild state it seems to me unreasonable to expect to alter the monogamous habit of the grouse.

Doubtless it is as well to have a preponderance of hens because they are subject to more risks than the cocks. There is considerable loss, for example, of sitting hens from predatory animals. But the proportions of the sexes should not be unduly disturbed by preferential shooting until we have more definite knowledge of the inclination, if any, to polygamy in grouse, and what the rearing results were on such a moor.

How many people take the trouble to ascertain the proportions of the sexes of grouse and partridges after each day's shoot? Certainly a few do. Much interesting biological knowledge could be built up over a period of years if such things as sex, age, weight, plumage state and so on were noted carefully after each shoot. Many an interesting example of aberrant plumage has been sent to the poulterer for lack of a critical eye over the bag. Over a period of years and in a haphazard way I have noted the sex from the plumage of 2851 partridges shot; the result was 1588 cocks and 1263 hens. In these figures there were several records of more hens than cocks in a day's shoot. The biggest disparity of this kind was of 72 cocks and 88 hens, shot on 14th October 1918, at Stanhoe in Norfolk. Conversely, the biggest proportion of cocks to hens was 44 to 29 on the same shoot on 18th October 1919.

I once used to see a covey of partridges so close that it was easy to tell the sexes. They used to feed in the snowy weather a few feet from the house windows. There were five of each sex. The size of the chestnut patch on the breast of partridges, commonly called the " horseshoe," is not an infallible sex test. The majority of cocks have this patch more fully developed than the hens, but sometimes a cock will have a very small horseshoe and a hen a very large one. The feathers on the scapulars should be the test.

In the cock these feathers are yellowish brown in ground colour, with very fine wavy black lines running across the feather, and with a chestnut-coloured patch towards the outside edge of the feather. These feathers in the hen are black in ground colour as far as the basal half is concerned, and across this are about two cross-bars of light yellow, and only towards the tips of the feathers are the fine wavy vermiculations found.

Both sexes have the light yellow longitudinal streak down the centre of the feather. The upper surface of the cock, therefore, appears yellow and red and that of the hen black and yellow. This is quite unmistakable. The cock partridge is more uniformly coloured and the hen more conspicuously variegated.

Many books nowadays make the mistake of suggesting that the wing coverts show these differences and should therefore be used for determining the sex; but, in fact, the markings on these feathers are not constant and are liable to be similar in both sexes.

Many hen partridges, especially in Norfolk, have no chestnut feathers in the horseshoe, this colour being replaced by white, but I have never seen a cock with a wholly white horseshoe. I have one in my collection which is nearly so, and I have heard of it being observed in two birds by friends.

Partridges take on an eclipse plumage of the head and neck in summer. In the cock the red feathers on face and forehead are replaced by paler feathers of sandy-red hue, and the blue-grey neck feathers are replaced by pale brown feathers with a small light streak down the centre of each feather. They are very like those of the fledgling plumage before moulting, though not so long and narrow, and the light streak is less conspicuous. In the hen bird the neck feathers are ornamented with quite a conspicuous white spot in place of the small streak in the cock bird.

Hungarian partridges, judging from the few I have handled, are much greyer than British birds, especially the hens.

The words " barren " and " mule " are often used by shooting men without regard to their proper meaning A pair of partridges or grouse that have lost their brood should not be called barren, nor should a hen pheasant that is assuming cock's plumage be termed a mule, which means a hybrid or cross. This abnormal plumage is caused by accident to, or atrophy of, the ovary.

When, in black game (*Lyrurus tetrix britannicus* With.), a grey hen is spoken of as a barren hen, the word is used aright, and of course all barren hens should be shot. But here again is the difficulty of knowing a barren hen when you see it, for even in the hand there is no difference between young and old, once the full plumage has been attained in the autumn of the first year.

Many people say shoot all single hens as they are old ones, but coveys are often broken up, so there is plenty of room for mistakes. As a rule one is requested to shoot only cocks, but sometimes single hens are also allowed : now when a wood is being driven some old hens may accidentally come over as an apparent small pack, and equally some young hens would be separated and come over as single birds.

Undoubtedly black game are decreasing in numbers in Britain and have been doing so for some time past. Professional forestry interests definitely discourage these birds. With its communal type of display among the males at the " lek," it is probable that once the numbers have been reduced below a certain limit, the full display cannot be completed nor breeding condition attained. This view was put forward by Fraser Darling in *Bird Flocks and the Breeding Cycle*, and the extinction of the heath hen in the eastern United States, despite the thousands of dollars spent to keep the species going, would seem to support this view.

There is no doubt we kill quite a few black game by accident during grouse drives. Everyone is liable to make the mistake now and then, often at the beginning of the season ; and the most confusing thing is when a mixed lot of grey hens and grouse come over together.    Some people have remarkably quick powers of discrimination.    The Mann family, with whom I have shot for well over forty years, can, and frequently do, pick out and kill cock partridges from driven coveys when the light is good.

Dr Percy Lowe sends me this letter on the subject of decrease of black game :—

During the last 50 or 70 years or more many people get up to Scotland for the shooting who would never have taken part in the old days.  These folk, when out for a day's " walking up," are unable to distinguish a grey hen from a grouse.  The consequence is that in spite of a stentorian cry of " grey hen " from the head-keeper, down comes the grey hen.  It is the duffer's chance.  No one could miss it or does as it rises from the bracken or rushes along the bottom of a " bank " or " side." I have seen it done time after time.

Another reason for their decline is the draining of the " slacks " which used to come down from the top of the same " side " in a regular sequence.  This was done for the sake of the sheep, but as the " slacks " are the favourite places for the black game to feed, the result was disastrous.  The late Sir Frederic Johnstone, who had the best black game shooting in Scotland after the Duke of Buccleuch, told me he was sure this was one of the surest ways of accounting for their dangerous decrease in numbers.

He said in some of the bottoms or vales you could see in the old days as many as a hundred or more blackcock sitting together on the high ground above some farmhouse.  Nowadays you are lucky if you see twenty, as I can testify.

Partridges pair off as early as January in mild winters, so it is the custom when pheasant shooting in that month to be careful to leave such paired partridges alone and only shoot at partridges in coveys that may come over as well as the pheasants.    Although this is advocated by men who know a great deal more about partridges than I do, I would venture to suggest it is not always a wise policy.    Early nests are more likely to come to grief from insufficient vegetational cover, and as young partridges live entirely on insects for some time, too early hatching may find them hungry. The bulk of partridges in this country hatch in the last two weeks of June, at which time in England there is a lot of cold sunless weather and often heavy rain.    The herbage is soaking and insects are slow to hatch and the little partridges often die by hundreds. What we want at that time are light showers of rain with some good honest bursts of sunshine in between.

A lot of this " what is wrong with the partridges ? " talk, putting the blame on macadamised roads, artificial manure, and chickens on the stubble, is piffle.    It is all and only a question of *weather*.    Given a good series of good seasons of weather, we shall get consecutive good seasons of partridges.    This is my experience, at least, in Norfolk.

CAPERCAILLIE HEN, WITH NEST AND EGGS
Fairburn, Ross-shire.  May 15, 1927.

The red-legged partridge (*Alectoris rufa rufa* L.) is not indigenous to Britain, but was introduced from the Continent about 1770, since when it has flourished. It is most numerous in the eastern counties. In days gone by, when walking-up and shooting over dogs was more in vogue, it became generally disliked by shooting men. Its greater tendency to run than the common partridge caused the dogs to be liable to break their point and draw in too much. They used also to be accused of harrying the native partridge at nesting time, with what truth I do not know. There are now very few places in England where partridges are shot over dogs, and the red-legged species is excellent for driving, flying straight and fast and not jinking when suddenly confronted by the line of guns, which is often a disconcerting habit of the "grey birds." But they soon get tired, especially on a wet day when their feet get heavily clogged with mud.

They are by no means restricted to the breck country in East Anglia, but are well distributed through the arable country. I have seen 132 red-legs included in a day's shoot of 343 partridges at Brancaster, Norfolk, and on an adjoining beat the following day there were 126 red-legs in a bag of 333 partridges. This was in October of the good partridge season of 1934, and these are the largest bags of red-legs I know.

There is a curious erythristic variety of the common partridge which used to be thought a distinct species and was called the mountain partridge (*Perdix montana*), but it is now known to be only a colour variety. Specimens have been shot in a good many counties in England at various times. The only one I ever saw was hanging up in Leadenhall Market. This bird being fresh and a handsome specimen, I bought it for my collection. I remember seeing a case with three of these birds at Hugh Whistler's house at Battle, Sussex, and if I remember aright, he told me they were all shot out of the same covey in that neighbourhood.

There is another variety of the common partridge in which all the chestnut colour in the normal bird is replaced by a dull yellow. I shot one in Lincolnshire but my host annexed it for his collection. A few days later we were driving the same shoot again, and I was in the same position as before. Only one covey came to me, out of which I shot one bird which was in more or less similar plumage.

It is rather surprising that the capercaillie (*Tetrao urogallus urogallus* L.) has no place in our game laws. It may possibly be that its reputed destructiveness to young growing fir trees has put it outside the pale of a protective close season—or is it that between 1760 and 1837 the bird was extinct and was disregarded as game?

It is essentially a forest-dwelling bird, and the eighteenth century was a time of extensive felling of the old forests of the Highlands. The period of its reintroduction coincided with a large amount of replanting, and the bird is now well distributed in the Eastern and Central Highlands and is found occasionally in many other parts of Scotland.

Their flight is swift and very powerful, the primary feathers being noticeably upturned at the tips from the pressure of air under them. Though gliding with motionless wings when coming down to settle, there is a great noise of air through the wings. There is also much noise when a capercaillie leaves the trees— nearly as much crashing as a bear would make. They will fly high into the air when flushed from trees on a steep hillside ; I have myself seen three huge cocks and two hens flying 300 feet over my head while I was futilely waiting below with my gun.

One should shoot well forward at a capercaillie, for being so big and apparently flapping so slowly they are deceptive as to pace. I once saw a very fine shot miss two capers in succession, and that at easy range.

Both capercaillie and black game are much disliked by foresters, but it is doubtful if they are now in sufficient numbers to cause serious trouble. Black game are not so restricted in diet, for in winter they feed largely on birch catkins.

Sometimes capercaillie make sudden movements into fresh territory, and when this happens it is the females which move first, to be followed by the cock birds the next year. It is quite common to find that in the first breeding season in their new place they will mate with blackcocks and produce hybrids.

I have often wondered why British sportsmen do not take more to rifle shooting in winter—in Scotland at any rate, where stalking cock capers and old blackcocks would surely give first-rate sport. When I was in Norway in 1899 with the late Johnny Millais, in the Gröndalen, his elk hunter, Kristian, told us that he shot many capercaillie in winter with his rifle. He would spy for them with a telescope as they sat on the tops of fir trees and then he would stalk them to about a hundred yards. He said he got mostly cocks as the hens are in the thicker parts of the forest and do not show themselves. His biggest bag was fourteen cocks in one day with sixteen shots. He was most contemptuous of the continental habit of spring shooting of capercaillie at the lek.

On that trip to Norway I went after ptarmigan and willow grouse while Johnny Millais went after elk, for which he had taken out eight rights. The willow grouse were to be found on the lower slopes of the hills above the forest line which finished with a belt

SNOWY OWL MOBBED BY RAVENS
Norway.

of birches. This open ground was covered with berry plants, such as blaeberry and crowberry, scrubby heather and patches of small sallows and birch. The ptarmigan were on higher ground still, among the stony tops. Here, too, there was always a plentiful supply of berry plants, with dwarf birch that crawled flat against the rocks like ivy. The few ptarmigan I came across were very wild, quite unlike our Scottish birds which sit about almost as tame as poultry. As a rule the only chances I got were when coming round rocky corners. When flushed they speedily got out of sight or plumped straight down hill. The most I ever shot in a day was five ptarmigan and one willow grouse, and on another day I got four ptarmigan and four willow grouse. These gave me an interesting set of skins showing different plumages. We always used the carcasses for food and they were a welcome change from elk meat which was our staple dish, but even a willow grouse, so close a relative of our British grouse, has nothing like the excellent flavour of our bird.

On those trips on the high ground I was always rather afraid of getting lost in the mist, but luckily there was no mist all the time I was there. A sprained ankle might have had serious consequences, as in that wild country there were no houses or people within miles and nobody knew when I started off which direction I might take. During the whole time of my wanderings I never came across a human being. The clear weather enabled me to take bearings when necessary.

I find among the notes I made at the time that the crops of ptarmigan contained leaves of birch and sallow and tops and leaves of crowberry (*Empetrum nigrum*); and from willow grouse I got leaves and berries of blaeberry (*Vaccinium myrtillus*), leaves and young catkins of birch, heather tops (*Calluna*) and crowberries.

I saw only one blackcock the whole time and that one I shot; his skin is in my collection. He was fairly well on with his moult (18th September), but there were still a good many of his eclipse neck feathers in position. The new black feathers that were coming in were growing from the same root as the brown feathers before the latter were shed—shoving them out as it were, so that many of the brown feathers were still sticking on to the ends of the new black ones.

I never saw many capercaillie, though there must have been a lot in this vast forest region. One day—very wet rain the whole time—I spent seven hours in the forest and saw only three, all of which flushed from the ground too far away to give chance of a shot. But there were other interesting birds to be seen, such as

K

a hawk owl, a goshawk and an eagle owl. There was a great dearth of small bird life in those interminable forests of pines. I saw small parties of Siberian jays, fieldfares, bramblings, marsh tits, and long-tailed tits of the northern white-headed species. Once I saw a robin and another day a hedge-sparrow. On the open ground above the forest line there were a few rough-legged buzzards, an occasional merlin and a few wheatears.

Hawk owls were very confiding as a rule, and on seeing me would come flying up and settle on a bare dead tree-top as if they wanted to investigate the monster invading their domain. I could then walk up to the tree while they sat there looking down at me, and make sketches of them at my leisure. They sit upright, but as a rule with their tail horizontal, not hanging down like a hawk's, and with their lower body and flank feathers fluffed out over their feet and wings. The primary feathers were held sometimes above and sometimes below the tail.

While making skins of two Siberian jays, I found they have a curious gland on the inside of the lower jaw, full of yellowish fatty stuff which was not particularly sticky. It looks exactly like the sticky gland which woodpeckers have in that position.

Before I close this section on game birds I should like to mention that instinctive habit, common among many ground-nesting species, of what is often called " injury-feigning " when the bird is flushed from the nest containing a brood. The late Eliot Howard used often to discuss this kind of subject with me, and his opinion as one of the great authorities on avian mentality ought to be placed on record, as I do not think he ever expressed himself on the subject in his books. His opinion was that the " injury-feigning " reaction was a confusion caused by the conflict of two strong urges, one to escape from immediate danger and the other to stay and protect the brood. This proceeding doubtless does have the effect of enticing an enemy such as a fox, stoat or cat away from the brood and therefore has a survival value, but let us not think a partridge has any true cunning in its mind when flapping away in this manner.

### III.   PHEASANTS

Although the pheasant (*Phasianus colchicus* L.) is shot in scores of thousands every season, there still appears a certain amount of confusion among those who shoot them as to what particular races of pheasants are represented. This is not surprising for the several races hybridise freely, so much so that the game farmers lay themselves out to produce the crosses of the races with a view to getting the best quality of pheasant for shooting purposes.

Without going too much into the details of plumage of these various races, a few notes on their chief characteristics might be helpful for identification.

Five different types have been introduced to Britain, one in such small numbers, however, that it seems to have left no mark —at least I have never found any trace of it.

The five races are as follows : the black-necked (otherwise English) pheasant (*Phasianus colchicus colchicus*), Chinese ring-necked pheasant (*Phasianus c. torquatus*), Mongolian pheasant (*Phasianus c. mongolicus*), Prince of Wales pheasant (*Phasianus c. principalis*) and the Japanese green pheasant (*Phasianus c. versicolor*).

The black-necked pheasant is a dark golden-brown coloured bird with no white ring on its neck ; it has yellowish brown wing coverts, dark purple-red rump feathers with purplish and green reflections. This race is indigenous to the neighbourhood of the Black and Caspian Seas, and is the most westerly race of all the pheasants. It was possibly introduced into Britain by the Romans—at least it is mentioned in a manuscript a hundred years before the Norman Conquest.

The Chinese ring-neck is a very light-coloured bird, the plumage on flanks and upper part of back being pale straw yellow ; the wing coverts are bluish grey, the rump light bluish or greenish, margined with a fringe of rusty orange, and the neck has a broad white collar.

The Mongolian pheasant is very dark, almost maroon coloured on the upper parts, more golden on the flanks, dark maroon on the rump, and the whole plumage has a dull greenish sheen on it. The wing coverts are white and the bird has a large white collar.

The Prince of Wales pheasant is the most whole-coloured of them all, being chestnut in colour from neck to tail. The rump is the same without any brilliant reflected colour, and there is no white ring. The bird is also distinguished by having all its breast and body feathers tipped with deep velvety brown, the usual black tips being retained only on the sides of the breast and flanks.

The Japanese green pheasant has the whole of the breast and flanks bottle green ; the back is greenish and purple bronze, shading down to greenish grey on the rump and wing coverts. There is no white on the neck.

In those countries where pheasants are indigenous, there are many more races and intermediate types to the number of about thirty, but the five mentioned are the only ones which have been turned down here for sporting purposes. By far the greater number of our acclimatised birds are hybrids between the old black-neck and the ring-neck which was imported about 150 years ago. I can remember when it was practically impossible to see a thoroughbred bird; it is by no means safe to say that because a pheasant has no trace of a white ring he is a genuine black-neck. The ring-neck blood is very potent and shows often in the rump feathers alone, which instead of being deep purple maroon are mixed with mottlings of yellow and green.

I think it may be said that present-day pheasants consist entirely of black-neck, ring-neck and Mongolian blood. The Prince of Wales seems to have quite died out, and I think the Japanese has also. This latter bird was thought much of when first brought here, but it is much smaller than any of the others and the strain was weak. When first crossed with the Mongolian it made a magnificent bird, large and handsome in colouring. It was a shy breeder, however, as a hybrid, and seems to have quite gone now.

Game farmers have in recent years imported large numbers of thoroughbred specimens of the three races—black-neck, ring-neck and Mongolian—from their native countries so that breeding can now be controlled. It is therefore common to-day to see several thoroughbred birds in a day's bag.

Some of our English-bred ring-necks are much lighter in colour than birds shot in China, the golden-straw colour extending over all the back and even the chestnut colour of the scapulars being replaced by it. This makes them conspicuous in flight.

The hen birds of the several races are practically all marked the same, the only slight difference being in the amount of black in the feathers. This distribution of black pigment is greatest in the Japanese hen and least in the Mongolian. The colour of the eyes of Japanese and Mongolian pheasants is light yellow instead of the dark golden-brown characteristic of the other races.

There is much variation in the plumage of pheasants, arising as genetic "sports" from original stocks. Whole or partial albinism is quite common, and another not-uncommon sport is meaninglessly called the Bohemian pheasant; it has all the black markings of the normal bird but the ground colour of the plumage is pale cream.

Another notable variation is a melanistic mutant which a Japanese worker on birds has named *Phasianus c. tenebrosus*, quite without authority, as scientific names should not be bestowed on mutations. This bird seems to have turned up about twenty years ago. The cock birds are black with brilliant blue and green reflections, the green predominating on the upper surface. Some are variegated by having a rich reddsh copper hue on each side of the shaft of the feathers on breast and flanks. The predominant colour of the hen birds is a deep chestnut, heavily marked with black. The hens have been erroneously described as much resembling grouse in colour and markings, but on close examination it will be seen there is no likeness whatever, only the red colour tending to give a superficial likeness. The patterning of the hen's feathers is the same as in other hen pheasants. The chicks of this mutant are sooty brown or black, sometimes with yellowish white about the head, neck and breast.

At first the bird was hastily described as a throwback to Japanese type, but this was quickly disproved. Moreover, the late Lord Rothschild had had living examples of this variety from Norfolk as long ago as 1888—which I believe was before the Japanese pheasant was brought to England (see *Ibis*, 1930, pp. 314-320). The game farmers soon gave their attention to this remarkable variety and found that if black cocks were mated to red hens they bred true. Large numbers were bred and turned down, but after the first curiosity was satisfied, familiarity bred contempt and many shooting men came to the conclusion that they were not a welcome addition to our pheasant types. Some said they were bad fliers, so orders for them ceased and only occasional ones are seen now. There is a record in Marquess Hachisuka's *Variations among Birds* of a hen Japanese pheasant showing this melanistic mutation in the wild state.

I have already mentioned the frequent appearance of a hen pheasant assuming male plumage. But these birds lack spurs and have a much smaller amount of scarlet face wattle. The most complete example in my collection also lacks the large black tips to the feathers of the breast and flanks. The only hen pheasant I have seen which had spurs was a melanistic mutant putting on a slight amount of cock's plumage. I also have a very fine aviary-bred Japanese pheasant which has complete cock's plumage.

A much rarer thing to come across in a day's shooting is a cock bird assuming hen's plumage. I have only seen two examples, both shot on Sir Edward Mann's Norfolk estate and very kindly given to me. One is now in my collection and the other at the Natural History Museum. All these aberrant birds in my collection have had their sex correctly determined while in the flesh by competent authorities, from examination of the reproductive organs.

Pheasants continue to retain their wildness even in and after a spell of captivity, and the many thousands of birds hand-reared under hens are soon quite wild and fly as well as those naturally bred in the coverts. They trust to their running powers when first disturbed, especially the cocks, and many a pheasant has escaped having to fly before the beaters by nipping into a ditch or hedgerow. Pheasants fly well from flat ground and give high sporting shots, such as often occur when root fields are being driven for partridges.

Under what circumstances does a pheasant present the most difficult shot? This question is often asked and there are several opinions. I should say one of the hardest shots is a high pheasant driven out of a cover to just within range and then curling round to go back again instead of keeping to his original course. Another very difficult shot is a bird slanting steeply from the summit of his flight. Cock pheasants are harder to hit than hens, and this is probably due to the deceptive effect of size on pace of flight.

There is a feature in the plumage of game birds which I have not seen mentioned in any book—the fact that the outer secondary feather is only about half the length of the adjoining and all the other secondary feathers. This can be verified in all the British game birds—capercaillie, black game, grouse, ptarmigan, partridge, red-legged partridge, quail and pheasant. It also occurs in the following pheasants: Amherst, golden, silver, Reeves', Elliot's, Swinhoe, impeyan, fire-back, crossoptelon, blood, peacock and Japanese glittering; and in tragopan, jungle fowl, koklas, bearded partridge, Californian quail, Virginian quail, francolin ruffled grouse and prairie hen.

I have not discovered it in very dry skins of sand grouse, but these are more allied to pigeons than game birds, and it is not to be seen in pigeons. So far I have not had the opportunity of examining peacock, turkey, bustard and guinea-fowl. It would be interesting to have expert comment on this characteristic of the short outer secondary feather.

**BULLFINCHES**
Feeding on Sorrel.

# PART V

## SOME OBSERVATIONS ON PAINTING BIRDS

This is not an easy subject to write about and must not be approached with assurance or dogmatism, as every one who studies art has his own ideas and methods and, quite rightly, follows and uses them in order to get the results that appeal to him.

Entirely different methods produce good results, and who shall say this or that is the right way? Individualism is necessary in all branches of art—if only to do away with monotony. It is to be supposed that " modern " artists would say that painting birds is not art at all, only " copying from nature." But those who have given their lives to painting pictures of birds will say that few things in nature are more beautiful and full of grace than birds : therefore, why not " copy " them? Especially so when one has the sense to realise how very difficult it is to copy a living bird.

You cannot requisition a living bird and direct it to sit for you in a certain pose for a long time as you can a human model. You are entirely dependent upon whatever attitude the bird happens momentarily to adopt, and you may never see a bird in just the pose you would like to represent it. Suppose you want to paint a picture of half-a-dozen ravens mobbing a pair of golden eagles. You would have to wait a long time to see such an event at all, though I saw it one day and remember it particularly, because it was while I was stalking my first stag on Ardlussa Forest, Jura, on 22nd September 1905. Now, even seeing this incident, there was no possible chance of " copying " it, for the birds' movements were far too rapid for the eye to register. But if you were clever enough and knew sufficient about the anatomy of the birds and were a good enough draughtsman, you might evolve a satisfactory picture. Knowing your birds well enough you might paint the picture without having seen the event. It is the *drawing* of the subject that is so difficult, especially of birds in violent action.

It is not easy merely to draw the profile of a bird in correct proportion gracefully and properly balanced on its feet. But having done that, it is easy enough to make a correct map of its plumage. There are so many species of birds that a large collection of skins is necessary, from which to work. This is what is generally wanted for purely the scientific illustration of birds. But painting pictures is a different matter. A great deal more knowledge is needed and a far greater power of draughtsmanship. The drawing of birds in movement demands not only the ability to represent foreshortening of the body, but also of the markings on the plumage. In such cases a certain amount of impressionism is obviously necessary; in fact, in painting *pictures* a lot more impressionism might be practised. But that is not to say that one should in any way dispense with scientific accuracy.

As a matter of fact, preoccupation with scientific book illustration is a handicap—and a big one—to painting pictures : one tends to aim simply at producing nothing but an accurate map of a bird's plumage. I feel my own pictures have suffered by this.

In the old days—by which I mean the early days of my own career—there was a good deal of antagonism between science and art in the minds of the people who wrote scientific books about birds. Apparently the accurate mapping of a bird's plumage was the first and only thing required, except a preposterous mass of landscape intended to show the bird's natural habitat. I was even told by a very eminent ornithologist of those days that the great fault of Wolf's illustrations was that they were too " artistic "—Joseph Wolf—who was the greatest draughtsman of birds who ever lived, and, as I truly think, ever will live ! But I am glad to say that at the present day authors and publishers are much more appreciative of the fact that art and science need not be in antagonism.

An absolutely correct map of the pattern and colour of plumage is a *sine qua non* for a scientific work, especially as some species are so closely allied that the differences of their plumage are very slight. But granted all this, there is no reason why light and shade and reflected lights should be eliminated. Light and shade help to convey an accurate impression of reality. Too much background is to be deprecated for scientific work. Realistic *foreground*, in the immediate vicinity of the bird, yes, but let it fade away into a wash of suitable tone and colour. Let the objects in the foreground be in proper relation to the size of the bird ; let it be remembered that a blade of grass may be as tall as a snipe ; and that one frond of bracken may be larger than a pheasant.

There is a strong tendency to depict miniature foregrounds (which are easier to paint than ones of appropriate scale and character and take about a quarter of the time) and also miniature landscapes as a background. Sometimes these landscapes are hopelessly out of proportion in relation to the bird depicted and an entirely false impression of size is conveyed.

When you consider the matter it is surely preposterous to paint a ringed plover on the sand with its head towering above the horizon line, when in looking at the subject in life one sees only

SCOTTISH DEER FOREST : STAGS SEPARATING FROM HINDS

Eilanreach.

the few inches of sand and pebbles immediately round the bird and the horizon line a long way above the bird's head. In fact, the horizon will be on the level of the observer's eyes ; to see it on a level with the bird itself the spectator would have to lie down and have his eyes only a few inches from the ground instead of at a height of five or six feet.

It is extraordinary how easy it is to make pictures and illustrations with the birds out of proportion to their surroundings. I have certainly done it many a time myself. If a *landscape with birds in it* is to be the subject for a picture, then paint the landscape first and put the birds in afterwards, taking care to keep them in proportion. But if it is to be a *picture of birds*, paint the birds first and add just sufficient landscape and foreground to give verity to the size of the birds.

Let us take an example : if a covey of ptarmigan is to be painted, taking up a fair amount of the space available, the birds had better be right in the foreground with the stones or rocks on which they are drawn coming right out at the bottom of the picture. If done in this manner it will be possible to introduce a fair amount of landscape behind the covey, without putting the birds out of proportion. But if the stones on which the ptarmigan rest are placed farther back into the picture, and ground is shown between these and the bottom of the picture, then the birds will appear much too large. Let us picture to ourselves a reindeer standing alongside the ptarmigan we have drawn—and we shall find the beast overflowing the whole of our picture ! The avoidance of such a dilemma is quite easy, as I have tried to show.

Another phenomenon which frequently proves a stumbling block to the illustrator is the position of reflections on the surface of water in relation to the object reflected. The reflection of a bird flying over or swimming in calm water is exactly below it, and when correctly represented suggests to the spectator the position of the bird in space. In order to find this correct position it is necessary —in the case of a flying bird—to fix the point on the *surface* of the water above which the bird is situated ; the reflection should then be placed exactly the same distance below this line as the bird is above it. This will suggest its distance from the spectator and also its height from the water's surface. In a close view, especially if the bird is of any size, it may not be possible to show any reflection, as most of it would fall outside the lower margin of the picture. (See Fig. 1 overleaf.)

It is a curious fact also, that reflections of birds standing in water in the foreground are often painted much too short in relation to the height of the bird. The reflections, as I have said, should

L

reach exactly the same distance below the bird as its height above the surface of the water. Almost always, when beginning to paint in this style of subject, I fall into this error and have to correct it afterwards. I suppose the reason is that the dark mass

FIG. 1.—The small spots indicate the surface of the water immediately underneath the birds flying over.

of one tone and colour fills the eye to a much greater extent than do the varied colours of the plumage of the bird itself, and therefore appears to be sufficient, though it is not really so. I can think of no other reason why I so often make this mistake. (See Fig. 2.)

I suppose all landscape and animal painters make innumerable sketches direct from nature in order to have material for the surroundings and foundations of the pictures they paint.   When I was young and strong I used to do a good deal of work in oils, and I have many sketches done in various parts of the world from the Tropics to the Arctic regions.   I never hesitated to take out easel, canvas and painting gear in midwinter.   I would work all day with snow deep on the ground, or skate out on to the ice and paint away until I was too cold to work, and so had to stop and take a cruise around on my skates until circulation was good enough to allow me to continue work.

FIG. 2.

I remember when I was in Sweden about sixty years ago I used to take my gun as well as my painting things when I went on the lakes to paint ice subjects.   On one of these occasions, while skating round to get warm, I heard what I thought was a great-spotted woodpecker's note, and having my gun with me I waddled on to land without removing my skates and followed the cry which I still heard at intervals among the birches and firs.   While thus occupied I came across a green woodpecker and promptly annexed it before continuing my search for the other bird.   I soon came across him and shot him easily.   He turned out to be a white-backed woodpecker (*Picus leuconotus*) and the first of this species I had ever seen.   I was probably more pleased with the results of this diversion than of my sketching !

I had a bad habit in those early days of trying to make rather highly finished little pictures of these sketches, and to this end used to go out several times to work on the same thing.   This is a great mistake unless you can hit off exactly the same kind of weather at the same time of day as when you started.   Otherwise different atmospheric conditions will give totally different effects and, of course, as the sun alters in position as the day wears on, the effect of light and shade is constantly changing.   So by degrees I found it much better and safer for getting truth of effect to do as much as I could at one sitting, taking pencil notes if necessary of detail I might need, and using these as material at a later date.   But even so, I began to find it wearisome to lug oil-painting kit about for miles, especially in hilly country.   I found I could never cope with water colour, so gave it up years ago in favour of tempera for small pictures and book illustrations, and came to the conclusion that a pencil and a small-sized sketch book were really the best things to carry for sketching purposes.

The great advantage of this method is that you have the means of recording in your pocket, and multitudes of shorthand sketches can be done on almost any occasion.

At one time, when I used to be lucky enough to get invitations for grouse shooting, I used to make a practice of making rough pencil sketches of the view from every grouse butt I occupied. There was almost always a long enough wait before the grouse began to come; also, on bye days, I used to toil up the hills with my painting kit and make oil sketches of grouse country. I accumulated a lot of material by these means and have subsequently taken advantage of it. I used to do the same thing while deer stalking, for I found that more magnificent atmospheric effects were often seen on such occasions than when one went out intentionally to paint.

I cannot help thinking that to a " painter-chappie " (by which term I was always alluded to by the keeper of a friend of mine in Scotland) there must be far more interest in a day's shooting or stalking than there is to most people in the party, no matter how keen and proficient they may be. For me there is the interest of waiting and watching and trying to remember all the actions and shapes of the birds and beasts for future painting. This takes a good deal of concentrated effort but is well worth it for the wealth of observed fact it provides.

I remember once painting a small picture for the late Edwin Montagu of some driven grouse. This he criticised, saying that he thought I had made their necks too long. I told him he might be right, but as he was going to Scotland shortly to shoot grouse, I asked him to take special notice of the point. This he did, and when he came back he said that after what he had just seen, he now thought I had not made the necks long enough! This just shows how a painter is observing much closer than one who is only a sportsman. A grouse's neck is relatively longer than a partridge's—to be exact, it is 4½ inches long.

There are a lot of men who have shot all their lives and are yet quite incapable of intelligently criticising a picture of game birds— or of any other bird or beast. The silliest remark I ever heard in connection with this matter was that of a shooting man who said he had picked up hundreds of shot partridges but had never yet seen the flank feathers coming up over the wings. It is a pity he had not the inclination, which every sportsman should have, to observe and find pleasure in watching closely in life the birds and beasts of the chase. I have been fortunate in my hosts on grouse moor, partridge manor, and deer forest, for they have all had a keen interest in natural history.

Landscape sketching direct from nature was especially useful to me at the beginning of my career, as I had to live in London for thirty-nine years of my life. There was some advantage in this in the near proximity of the Zoo and the Natural History Museum, which gave me opportunities for studies I might not have been able to make elsewhere; but London is not a good place to live in when one wants to paint partridges on stubble fields, falcons on rocks and like things. I could get on with the partridges and falcons all right but had to trust to my sketches for stubbles and rocks. I used to go out into the parks at night and surreptitiously lift a few twigs and bits of foliage from which I was able to make suitable drawings of perches for my tom-tits! But this kind of material was restricted in variety and I had sometimes to write to the country for some rubbish or other to be sent to me by post. I repeat, however, that I never wasted my time when there was a chance to sketch from nature. I filled many sketch books with drawings in pencil of the varied growth of grasses and reeds, the way their leaves grow from the stems, the foreshortening of branches of trees—both towards and receding from the observer—the light and shade which emphasise foreshortening, clods of earth in a ploughed field, formation of clouds in the sky, rocks, stones and dead leaves. All these things drawn from nature are valuable when one comes to spend long spells in the studio.

I was always especially interested in rocks, and have numberless carefully drawn sketches, some in pencil and some in oils. Most of these have been done in Norway, Scotland and Ireland. Rocks near the sea have different kinds and colours of lichens on them and therefore need quite dfferent treatment from rocks on a mountain-side. The vegetation round different types of rock or cliff also needs most careful attention if a picture is to carry conviction.

Rocks are not easy to draw satisfactorily from imagination. Besides colour and vegetation there are such factors as textures, angles, cracks, strata, broken surfaces and so on, which are hard to visualise correctly enough to put on canvas unless you have had a lot of experience of close observation and sketched material.

It is useful to make a careful painting or drawing of a good big mass of rock; then you can make use of any small portion of it to copy for a stand for a falcon or other rock-haunting bird. In this way one useful sketch will provide material for perhaps a dozen pictures.

Rocks are not the only things to be studied in this way; trees and branches are equally important. A dead branch, foreshortened towards the spectator is a far more interesting perch for a sparrow-hawk or jay than a straight horizontal branch going across the picture. These details are important.

I have often heard and read that birds in the Zoo have a wretched and moped appearance and are not good subjects for pictures. From my own experience, which is a long one, I would say that a lot of such talk is nonsense. I have seen and drawn birds of many kinds there and have found the greatest benefit from being able to sketch from life at such close quarters. Looking through field glasses at wild birds is not half so good.

Some people think that a bird is of necessity moping if it sits quiet on its perch with its feathers rather fluffy. Probably it is merely digesting its last meal. This is especially so with raptorial birds which take a heavy meal and sit quiet naturally for a long period. A wild eagle or falcon does not spend its whole time soaring about the sky. A hide at nesting time would be the only way to get many studies of a resting eagle in nature, but the Zoo gives many opportuniies of getting several species of eagles in various postures. The same may be said of many other constantly painted British species, such as ducks, gulls, waders and small passerines, which can be studied in extraordinarily good conditions in the large flight aviaries at the Zoo. One can make no complaint either about the gloss and health of the plumage of most of them.

All this is not to say the bird painter should not be a bird watcher in the wild as well; and he must have his field glasses. The best kind to get are those of wide field, magnifying six, seven, or certainly not more than eight times. Good binoculars, which are light in weight and admitting a great deal of light, are expensive but an excellent investment.

A large magnification, which gives a small field, is not good, especially for close work with birds. It is difficult to hold the glasses still enough to prevent eye-strain; moreover, your bird is so apt to flit out of the field of vision. Once it has gone it is surprising how hard it is to pick it up again through the glass.

One of the difficulties of drawing birds is coping satisfactorily with foreshortened postures. The movements of birds, also, are so lively that it takes a very quick eye to see and know what one is looking at, and what a bird is really doing. The only way is to make sketches as rapidly as possible and afterwards make the best one can of a bad sketch. Errors can often be rectified at leisure without spoiling the freshness of the sketch from life. But never

GOLDCRESTS
On branch of Spruce Fir.

let it be said by the bird artist that such and such a thing must be right because it was done from life : I know the fallacy of this all too well. Sometimes a bird painter must make up his drawing in piecemeal fashion, doing a few strokes at a time until the detail of the movement is captured. I have in mind, for example, the intricacies of ducks displaying.

One has only to think how easily human eyesight is baffled by the quickness of such things as card tricks, thimble-rigging, and all other sorts of conjuring to appreciate how the rapid movements of birds can baffle the vision. How many people, for example, have observed that a canary or other small bird hopping from one perch to another in a cage, uses its wings to help itself across ? This opening and closing of the wings is so quick that it is invisible to any but an observer who has trained himself.

A celebrated bird painter had depicted in one of his books a golden-eye drake displaying. This bird is figured as lifting one of its feet clear of the water and shooting a spray away from the foot. Doubtless this is what appeared to happen to this exceptionally keen observer. But another may see and interpret this part of the display quite differently. I once spent a whole day watching displays of golden-eyes in company with the late Gerald Legge, on a cold and frosty day in spring. These were not wild golden-eyes, viewed from a long distance away ; we were observing them at close quarters. It was manifest to us that the spray of water spurting out from behind the bird was caused by the drake lifting his foot clear of the water and giving a violent kick downwards and backwards, thus causing the splash to come *from the surface of the water*. This is just one little incident to show how easily the eye can be misled and how one should hesitate to dogmatise on matters of natural history.

No doubt the modern developments of ultra-rapid photography will become increasingly useful in elucidating such matters as these, but in painting pictures of birds, photographs should be used with the greatest caution. I am thinking particularly of birds flying. Personally, I never use photography as a help ; I much prefer to do as much as I can with my own eyes. I have never taken a photograph in my life and, of course, would never dream of using anybody else's photograph. However erroneous one's effort may be, given some natural ability for the job, it is surely better to rely on one's own careful observation. The difference between a photographic record and an exact impression of rapid movement is erroneous. Rapid actions of birds and beasts should be rendered as they appear to the trained eye.

Take the very simple example of the wheels of a motor-car : we know there are spokes to the wheel and a photograph may show these even when the machine is travelling fast.  But the fact of showing them has the pictorial effect of eliminating entirely the illusion of movement.  We should never dream of painting in these spokes but should leave them blurred.

Galloping horses provide another example.  The innumerable photographic illustrations of racing and steeplechasing which one sees in illustrated papers show, no doubt, the horses as they are at one moment of time, but do not convey the impression of speed.  Compare these photographs (without questioning their value from a technical point of view) with pictures of horses in violent action, such as used to be painted by Lady Butler, Caton Woodville and others.  Here you will see all the violent strength and pace, clatter and rattle which are appreciated by the senses as a whole, instead of the subtle petrified accuracies that are recorded by the mechanical lens.  Blampied's etchings of horses racing certainly convey the impression of speed and the dust of cornering, but if you begin to look at the work line for line you wonder how on earth these scratches can give the idea of horse at all.

How, then, are we to paint flying birds ?  It is more difficult to get the impression of the speed of birds flying in the air than of animals running on the ground, the chief reason being that there is no visible displacement of air in a bird's progress ; whereas with animals on the ground there might be violent, visible displacement of solid material such as flying clods and smothers of sand and dust which may obliterate much of the detail of the beasts causing such a disturbance.

A bird soaring or skimming with motionless wings is much easier to paint than one in rapid flight, for then only a blur of wings is visible ; indeed, in the case of a humming bird hovering before a flower, we see no evidence of movement at all.  We know all about how the feathers clothe the wings, but if we paint in all these feathers with their colours and markings, we petrify the bird. On the other hand, if we paint the wings in a blur the result is a daub.  So what is to be done ?  It is no good giving the counsel of despair by saying don't paint flying birds.  Something must be sacrificed and a compromise made ; and each individual artist must be a law unto himself and solve the problem in his own way.

I once had a conversation on this very subject with the late E. Neale of how to get the idea of speed into a picture of flying birds, such as a covey of grouse.  I told him that to me a covey

A PAIR OF TIGERS

of grouse on the wing always conveyed the impression that each bird was doing exactly the same thing at the same time—I meant so far as the position of the wings is concerned, and that I should paint them accordingly. The monotony of this similar attitude would be broken by tilting some of the birds a little and placing some above and some below the eye—all of which would necessitate different methods of representing each bird's wings, although the main idea would be kept in view and all the birds would have their wings on the downward or upward stroke. This I thought helped to convey the idea of speed and movement. But he held an entirely different point of view and said his idea would be to paint the birds in as many different positions of flight as possible. There can be no hard and fast rules.

As a rule, stuffed mounted birds should never be used as models unless, indeed, one knows so much about the subject that the imperfections of the stuffing can be rectified in the drawing. No matter how well a bird may be stuffed—and there are few such—it will always lack the grace of the living bird. But stuffed specimens may come in useful for getting correct ideas of light and shade and reflected lights. They may also help in getting a proper drawing of foreshortening.

Place a grouse in three-quarters profile before you and you will find that drawing the foreshortening of the near wing does not merely consist of delineating the principal rows of feathers such as primaries, secondaries, secondary coverts and so on a little shorter than they would be if the bird were entirely in profile ; you will find rather that these rows of feathers, or some of them, according to the angle of the bird, have disappeared from view as the natural curve of the bird's contour slopes away from the eye's viewpoint. It will be found also that the markings of the plumage of a bird may be altered in shape entirely when seen obliquely.

For instance, a bird may have its flank feathers ornamented with crescentic markings, the concave position of the crescents being towards the forward part of the body. But when viewed from a position behind the bird, these crescents will be found to have reversed their appearance and are now to be seen with a new shape, the curvature being shown towards the tail end instead of towards the head. The correct drawing of this makes all the difference between a solid and a flat representation. A bird has no sharp outline ; its feathers and markings are subject to the subtlest modifications of shape and appearance when viewed from different points of view.

Although drawing from stuffed birds is to be deprecated, it is

M

essential to have a good many skins of various species, as it is quite impossible to get scientifically correct drawings of the intricate markings of plumage without skins for constant reference. It is impossible to do such drawings from life; the birds must be handled. Even at close quarters in the Zoo the intricate pattern of markings, such as on the females of many genera of the Phasianidæ, could not be done satisfactorily. Plain, simple things need most careful representation in a scientific drawing; for example, the white bar across the wing of a blackcock must be shown to be caused by the bases of some of the secondaries which are exposed beyond the tips of the secondary coverts, and not by the tips of the latter row of feathers which overlap the bases of the secondaries. Such accuracy would not matter and, indeed, would be deplorable in a picture where a flock of blackcock might be shown fairly small on a landscape.

It is useful to have some wings of birds preserved in extended positions, as a help in drawing correctly these in foreshortened positions. Drawing a widely spread wing in this position is no simple thing, nor to get the corresponding wing into the right position on the other side. Birds use their wings simultaneously, like a man using a pair of oars in a boat, except when they are turning.

I have sometimes found it helpful to make diagrams of a pair of outspread wings, cut out of cardboard. Some of these I have widely spread and others more flexed. I make these by drawing one wing in the position required, then allowing for the distance of half the breadth of back between the two wings, I double the piece of cardboard and cut out the wing with scissors. By this means I have a pair of wings which I can hold to any angle I wish for a drawing and have a rough guide (only a very rough guide, be it noted) to the relation of the wings to each other. Let me emphasise that being only a flat piece of cardboard this device gives no indication of the thickness of the wing, nor of the convexity of the upper surface and corresponding concavity below.

A collection of separate wings enables one to see the under plumage of the wing in a way ordinarily mounted skins do not permit. I have a good many wings for this purpose, and at one time I used to make elaborate life-sized drawings of the inside of wings done from birds in the flesh. These are useful to have at hand but take longer to do than preparing the real wings.

It may be asked why go to all this bother when you could have a few birds stuffed with their wings in flying position? This might be done and be useful up to a point, but I am dead against using stuffed birds as models. There is always the temptation to

MALLARD ON ICE

depend on them too much and copy their stiffness and rigidity. Personally, I would rather trust my eyesight and knowledge of birds. Such knowledge comes from much observation over a long period, and for the sake of learning more about how birds move and shape themselves I should like to have a few more hundred years of life. It is incumbent on us painters to study wild life direct as much as ever we can.

A general knowledge of pterylosis (the distribution of and growth of feathers on the bird) is indispensable. A profound knowledge is not necessary for the artist. It is an intricate subject for there is considerable variation in the different Orders of birds throughout the world. The artist must realise that feathers do not grow haphazard all over the body, but are confined to definite tracts with bare spaces of skin in between. A knowledge of the arrangement of these pterylæ is most helpful when doing illustrations for scientific books, especially if one has to work from bad dried skins. Skins made by collectors in the field are often poor, especially if they were obtained in the tropics, where speed in preparation is necessary. The feathers are in disarray and the patterning far from obvious. What may appear as spots on a poorly-made skin may be definite longitudinal bars in the living bird. The wings, which need such careful treatment, are often crumpled. To add to the difficulties of using skins of other people's making, one often finds the scapular feathers dragged under the back feathers and completely hidden from view and lost. This happens especially when the skinner has indulged the habit of tying the wing bones together (*i.e.* the wings to each other) and then fastening off with the wing joints close together over the back of the bird. Though it may make a neat skin it is an untrue one by reason of the loss of the scapulars.

Anatomy is also a helpful science, and the painter should know without doubt upon which bones of the wing the different lots of feathers lie. My own knowledge of anatomy and pterylosis has come entirely from my own investigations in the course of preparing skins.

Even in scientific illustrations it is possible to be artistic in the composition of the surroundings of the bird. If it is perched on a living twig it should be readily discernible what species of tree the bird is favouring.

You cannot paint birds successfully without scientific knowledge, by which I mean ordered knowledge. You must know the various stages of plumage for different seasons and stages of the bird's life history, and have the surroundings of the picture seasonable.

A golden eagle, for example, looks very nice when the plumage is at the period when the basal half of the tail feathers are white. But it would be quite wrong to paint eagles at the nest in this stage of plumage, as it is a sign of immaturity; and eagles do not breed until they are fully adult and have lost their white feathers.

There is sometimes a certain amount of antagonism between field naturalists and so-called museum naturalists. This should never be. The bird watcher often claims that a knowledge of the living bird is the important thing. But he is apt to forget that the vast number of birds all over the world cannot be intensively watched in the wild state; and if they could, but few of them would be identified and classified correctly. The results of collecting by field naturalists and classifying by the museum naturalists form the fine body of exact knowledge we have at present and which is available to all who care to read. The observers who decry collecting and yet treasure their illustrated bird books should remember that at least one painter owes his accuracy in part to collections of skins and birds in the hand.

Sometimes when painting I have found myself quite unable to draw a bird satisfactorily in the position I wished. After much ineffectual labour I found the best thing was to leave the problem and come back to it in a day or two; then, seeing it with a fresh eye it can often be tackled with success. During the stages of painting a picture I find it useful after a day's work to have the thing under constant observation—so that whatever I happen to be doing I can take a glance at it, or even just sit in front of it smoking a pipe. All sorts of little improvements then become manifest. A bit of bad drawing can be rectified, the composition improved, relative tones adjusted and so on. When actually painting one is concentrating on a limited part of the picture. This later contemplation gives a breadth of view and helps in " pulling the thing together."

If your observation and your memory are good and your imagination vivid, it is not necessary to stick rigidly to painting from nature. Think of a golden oriole—black and yellow— splendid colours. Why not paint a picture in black and yellow, not necessarily such vivid hues as the orioles? It is quite simple. A hazy late afternoon with an amber-coloured sky, a sort of hazy gold, a bit of straggling black hedge coming from the side of the picture and showing against the sky and disappearing over the ridge before reaching the other side of the picture. Sloping down from the hedge a field of dead, bleached yellow grasses, with a few stunted thorn bushes or gorse (a very few, just two or three) dotted here and there. There is the picture : if you want life in it put in (quite small) a single old crow. Or, rather in the foreground and to one side—the side from which the hedge is shown coming into the picture—you could, for the sake of composition, show a cock pheasant strolling about, or a fox on the prowl. The main subject of a picture—bird, beast, tree or clump of bushes—no matter what it is, should be so placed as to keep the eye inside of the picture, and the arrangement should be asymmetrical rather than symmetrical. That is my idea, at least, of composition, though that is a matter of individual opinion.

The best medium for painting birds for scientific book purposes is undoubtedly water colours, but it is quite impossible to get the intricate pattern of many plumages without having recourse to the use of body colour. As I have said, I always use tempera myself for book illustrations.

Tempera is an opaque medium, like oils, and cannot be used for clean transparent washes like water colour, but has to be used with the help of white and as a rule has to be worked with a very dry brush. The details of a bird's plumage can be got just as well in tempera as in water colour ; the effect is almost that of an oil painting. Tempera has the merit of drying very permanently so that one can paint in details over an already painted ground-work without disturbing the under-colour. To such an extent can this be done that I have painted an entirely different subject over a picture already done. Also, I have left a picture face downwards in a bath of water for an hour, in order to detach it from the mount, without a single particle of the colour being altered by running.

There is always a much more beautiful effect in a landscape when viewed from a point facing the sun. It is infinitely more delicate in colour and much less flat and monotonous in tone than when seen with the sun at your back. But it is often difficult to get on to canvas a correct impression of what one sees. I remember painting—or rather trying to paint—an expanse of heather in full bloom facing a low afternoon sun. It was sparkling and beautiful to see, but was so grey that I could only make it look as if it were covered with hoar frost. When looking at that view, there was the knowledge *in my mind* that I was seeing a mass of lilac-coloured heather and therefore the lack of the colour in this momentary effect of light was not missed. But it was quite otherwise with the attempted painting. Every one knows what a beautiful effect is to be seen when looking at a flock of sheep or a herd of deer from a position facing the sun—each beast in a deep tone of shadow with a brilliant golden halo touching the top of their backs. This effect can also be given to birds in a picture, but not in a book illustration where the subject must be in full light and showing details of plumage.

For me, it is far more interesting to paint pictures than to illustrate scientific books. But as the latter are numerous and necessary, let us have as much art in them as possible in order to offset some of the extreme crudities of science. This, at least, is my philosophy.

It had always been my wish, given the time and opportunity, to illustrate completely a book on British birds. That wish, I hope, may some day be fulfilled, for in conjunction with David Bannerman, who will be responsible for the subject-matter, *A History of British Birds* is now in preparation, for which I have painted 330 full-page illustrations in colour. In carrying out this part of our project I have had an opportunity to practise what I have preached in this chapter of *Memoirs of an Artist Naturalist*. The text will be written in narrative style, not in the form of a reference work, and in no sense is intended as a rival to Witherby's *Handbook*, which will remain an indispensable encyclopedia of facts for all time. It is our hope, rather, that we may jointly produce a readable book which is out of the ordinary, and that both text and illustrations will appeal to the increasingly wide public who find relaxation in art and in the scientific study of bird life.

# GLOSSARY OF HAWKING TERMS

*Bate :* a hawk " bates " when struggling to fly from fist or block.

*Bind :* to clutch and hold the quarry in the air, instead of giving it a knock-out blow.

*Blue hawk :* a peregrine in adult " blue " plumage.

*Check :* to " check " is to leave the quarry flown at for another.

*Eyass :* a young hawk taken from nest.

*Falcon :* female peregrine or gyr. Also applied to other long-winged falcons, such as Saker, Lanner, Shahîn, etc.

*Foot :* a hawk is a good or a bad " footer " according to her ability or otherwise to hit or to catch her quarry.

*Hack :* young hawks taken from nest are kept at " hack," which is complete liberty until the time that they must be put into training.

*Haggard :* a wild-caught hawk in adult plumage.

*Intermewed :* a hawk that has moulted in captivity.

*Jack :* the male merlin.

*Jesses :* the short leather thongs that are permanently fixed to the hawk's legs.

*Lure :* a leather pad garnished with a couple of wings, tossed into the air at end of a line, used to bring down hawks to the falconer after unsuccessful flight ; also used for training purposes.

*Man :* to man a hawk is to make it tame. A well-" manned " hawk will sit quietly on fist, unhooded, showing no fright or distrust of strange sights and noises.

*Merlin :* the female merlin.

*Musket :* the male sparrowhawk.

*Out of the hood :* flying a peregrine, or other long-winged hawk, direct from the fist at quarry.

*Passage hawk :* a hawk caught wild in its immature plumage.

*Pitch :* the height that a hawk attains in the air while " waiting on."

*Put in :* a quarry " puts in " to cover to escape pursuing hawk.

*Plume :* a hawk " plumes " her quarry when plucking it.

*Quarry :* the game flown at.

*Rake away :* a hawk leaving its quarry and flying away.

*Red hawk :* a peregrine in its immature plumage.

*Sparrowhawk :* female sparrowhawk.

*Stoop :* the downward plunge of a hawk on to its quarry.

*Tiercel*, or *tercel :* the male of peregrine or gyr, and kindred long-winged hawks.

*Truss :* same as to " bind."

*Waiting-on :* a hawk circling overhead waiting for quarry to be flushed.

*Weather :* hawks on their blocks in the open air are " weathering."

There are many more technical falconry terms ; but the above will suffice for this book.

# GALLERY OF ARTWORK

The artist at work in his Camberley studio, 1947.
The finished painting can be seen overleaf at the beginning of the Gallery.

## AN INTRODUCTION TO THE GALLERY

George Edward Lodge has left behind a prolific and varied selection of artwork for us all to enjoy. His work has the ability to educate and teach us something special about nature's wonderful realm.

Lodge was far more interested in portraying birds and wildlife in picture form, rather than illustrating scientific books. However, as the latter were numerous and necessary he would have them contain as much art as possible in order to "offset some of the extreme crudities of science". That, at least, was his philosophy.

This gallery demonstrates the versatility of Lodge's artistic skills, and his unrivalled ability to portray what he knew and saw. These qualities derived from an insatiable enthusiasm for the subject and superb powers of observation.

G.E.L. Trust

Adult Greenland gyr-falcon.
Oil on canvas.

Great black woodpecker, *The Birds of the British Isles*, vol. IV plate 13.
Tempera.

Ptarmigan just alighted on a mountain-side scree.

Tempera.

'Sylvia', an eyass peregrine falcon on a grouse (see *Memoirs* pages 4 & 5).
Tempera.

Albino white-tailed sea eagle, North Roe, Shetland, 1915 (see *Memoirs* pages 36 & 37). Oil on canvas.

Golden eagle carrying a red deer calf (see *Memoirs* page 38).
Tempera.

Highland red deer stag.
Oil on board.

English partridges in winter landscape, 1888.
Oil on canvas.

Red squirrels at their drey.
Tempera.

Adult goshawk on forest edge.
Tempera.

Golden orioles, *The Birds of the British Isles, vol.1 plate 12*.
Tempera.

Willow tits, *The Birds of the British Isles*, *vol.11 plate 28*.
Tempera.

Peregrine and stoat, "Mutual Astonishment". Tempera.

Here again the falconer's eye and the painter's hand have conspired to produce a picture which could not be bettered for detail, both of anatomy and plumage. The poise of the bird and the pert defiance of the stoat are masterly.

Merlin with a skylark.
Tempera.

Deer stalking in the Highlands, Eilanreach, Glenelg.
Tempera.

Norwegian elk.
Oil on canvas.

Hawks weathering. Tempera.

The falconer has to spend considerable time in the training and care of his charges if he is to enjoy good sport. Open country, such as downland and moors, is the ideal setting and it is in these districts that hawking still survives.

Thomas Mann's rook hawking party, Cambridgeshire, 1889 (see *Memoirs* page 7). Oil on canvas.

*Thomas Mann stands by the hawking cadge holding 'Vic', a peregrine falcon. Mann's professional falconer, Alfred Frost, kneels at the cadge. George Lodge is seated on the ground, to the right, smoking his pipe. Both Mann and Lodge are wearing the green coats of the Old Hawking Club.*

Mallards.
Tempera.

A woodcock among reeds.
Tempera.

# FROM GEORGE LODGE'S FIELD SKETCH BOOKS

Lions at London Zoo, 1880s or 90s.
Pen and ink.

Tiger at London Zoo, 1880s or 90s.
Pen and wash.

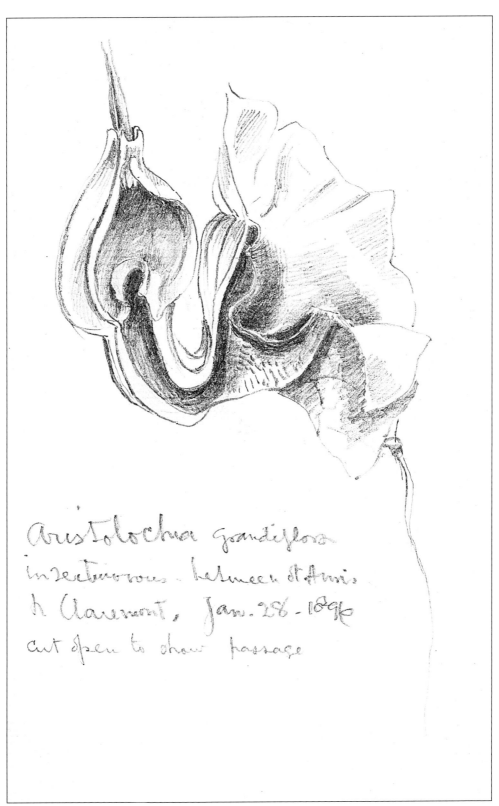

Aristolochia grandiflora
insectivorous. between St Anis
& Claremont, Jan. 28. 1896
cut open to show passage

Aristolochia grandiflora, West Indies, 1896.
Pencil sketch.

Tawny owls, 1880s or 90s.
Watercolour.

Waxwing, 1880s or 90s.
Watercolour.

Long-tailed tits, 1880s or 90s.
Watercolour.

Greenland gyr-falcon, 1880s or 90s.
Watercolour.

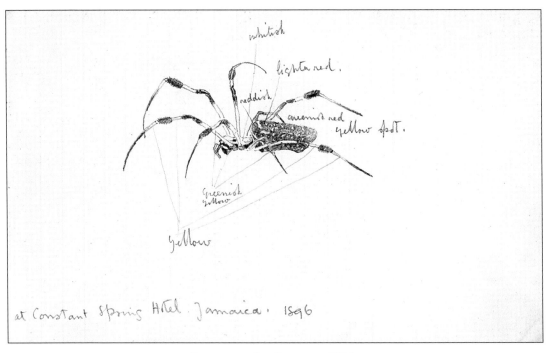

Banana spider, Jamaica, 1896.
Pencil study.

Lemming, Norway, 1899.
Pencil study.

Young fieldfares, Norway, 1900.
Pencil sketch.

Capercaillie.
Pencil sketch.

Ptarmigan hiding, Norway, 1902.
Pencil sketch.

Wasp's nest, Jamaica, 1896.
Pencil sketch.

Grouse on moorland, 1906.
Pencil sketch.

nose to be a little
thicker

Norwegian elk, 1899.
Pencil sketch.

mongoose

Mongoose, West Indies, 1896.
Pencil study.

Peregrine eyrie, 3 or 4 young fledged peregrines, 1906.
Pencil sketch.

3 young fledged peregrines.
Finished work from the sketch above.

# STONE LITHOGRAPH

Peregrine falcon in immature plumage.

Holm of Noss, Shetlands, 1914.
Oil sketch.

Red Banks, North Roe, Shetlands. Site of nest locality of the albino sea eagle, 1914 (see *Memoirs* page 36). Oil sketch.

# WOOD ENGRAVINGS

The silent pool, Albury, 1880.

Teal "put in" by tiercel peregrine.

Hobby and nest.

Woodcock ready to rise.

Kingfisher.

Wigeon on the snow.

# BIBLIOGRAPHY
## A GUIDE TO THE BOOKS, CATALOGUES AND JOURNALS CONTAINING ILLUSTRATIONS BY GEORGE E. LODGE

Falcon wing study by G.E. Lodge.

1. Aflalo, F. G. (1898) *A Sketch of the Natural History - Vertebrates - of the British Islands*
2. Baker, E. C. S. (1908) *The Indian Ducks and their Allies*
3. Baker, E. C. S. (1913) *Indian Pigeons and Doves*
4. Baker, E. C. S. (1921-1930) *The Game-birds of India, Burma and Ceylon*
5. Baker, E. C. S. (1922-1930) *Fauna of British India, Birds*
6. Bannerman, D. A. (1930-1951) *The Birds of Tropical West Africa*
7. Bannerman, D. A. (1953) *The Birds of West and Equatorial Africa*
8. Bannerman, D. A. and Lodge, G. E. (1953-1963) *The Birds of the British Isles*
9. Bannerman, D. A. and Bannerman, W. M. (1958) *Birds of Cyprus*
10. Bannerman, D. A. and Bannerman, W. M. (1963-1968) *Birds of the Atlantic Islands*
11. Bannerman, D. A. and Bannerman, W. M. (1971) *Handbook of the Birds of Cyprus and Migrants of the Middle East*
12. Bannerman, D. A. and Vella-Gaffiero, J. A. (1976) *Birds of the Maltese Archipelago*
13. Baxter, E. V. and Rintoul, L. J. (1953) *The Birds of Scotland*
14. Beebe, C. W. (1918-1922) *A Monograph of the Pheasants*
15. Beebe, C. W. (1926) *Pheasants, their lives and homes*
16. Bird, B. F. ed. G. E. L. Trust (2009) *George Edward Lodge: An Artist's Perspective on Falconry*
17. Bird, B. F. ed. G. E. L. Trust (2010) *George Edward Lodge: Artist Naturalist and Falconer, 150th Anniversary Exhibition of Artwork and Memorabilia*
18. Bosworth-Smith, R. (1905) *Bird Life and Bird Lore*
19. Bryden, H. A. (1930) *Enchantments of the Field*, Chronicles of Sport and Wild life
20. Chapin, J. P. (1932-1954) *Birds of the Belgian Congo*
21. Christy, R. M. (1890) *The Birds of Essex*
22. Coape-Oates, W. (1905) *Wild Ducks: How to rear and shoot them*
23. Coombes, R. A. H. (1952) *Mountain Birds*
24. Corballis, J. H. (1891) *Forty-Five Years of Sport*
25. Coward, T. A. (1920 - new edn, 1950) *The Birds of the British Isles and their Eggs*
26. Cox, H. E. and Lascelles, Hon. G. W. (1892 - new edns) *Coursing and Falconry* (Badminton Library)
27. Crawfurd, O. ed. (1895) *A Year of Sport and Natural History*
28. Darling, F. F. (1943) *Wild Life of Britain* (Britain in Pictures Series)
29. De Chamerlat, C. A. (1987) *Falconry and Art*
30. Drewitt, Hon. Mrs C. M. (1900) *Lord Lilford: A Memoir by his Sister*

31. Evans, A. H. (1899) *Birds* (Cambridge Natural History Series, Vol. IX)
32. Fisher, J. M. M. (1942) *The Birds of Britain* (Britain in Pictures Series)
33. Fleming, Sir C. A. (1983) *George Edward Lodge: The Unpublished New Zealand Bird Paintings*
34. Ford, E. (1999) *Gyrfalcon*
35. Gathorne-Hardy, Hon. A. E. (1914) *My Happy Hunting Grounds*
36. Geikie, Sir A. (1916) *The Birds of Shakespeare*
37. Glasier, P. E. B. (1978 - new edns) *Falconry and Hawking*
38. Gossard, (1973) *An Approved Treatise of Hawkes and Hawking*, facsimile copy of the 1619 original
39. Graham, P. A. (1895 - new edn, 1908) *Country Pastimes for Boys*
40. Greene, W. T. (1898) *Birds of the British Empire*
41. Harting, J. E. (1891 - new edns) *Bibliotheca Accipitraria, A Catalogue of Books Ancient and Modern Relating to Falconry*
42. Harting, J. E. (1898 - new edns) *Hints on the Management of Hawks, To Which is Added Practical Falconry*
43. Harting, J. E. (1898 - new edns) *The Rabbit* (Fur, Feather and Fin Series)
44. Harting, J. E. (1906) *Recreations of a Naturalist*
45. Hartley, G. W. (1903) *Wild Sport with Gun, Rifle and Salmon Rod*
46. Hartley, G. W. (1912) *Wild Sport and Some Stories*
47. Hollom, P. A. D. (1952) *The Popular Handbook of British Birds*
48. Hollom, P. A. D. (1960) *The Popular Handbook of Rarer British Birds*
49. Howard, H. E. (1929) *An Introduction to the Study of Bird Behaviour*
50. Howard, H. E. (1940) *A Waterhen's World*
51. Howard, H. E. (1920 - new edn, 1948) *Territory in Bird Life*
52. Hubbard, E. ed. (1895) *Bird Notes by the late Jane Mary Hayward*
53. Hudson, W. H. (1895 - new edn, 1930) *British Birds*
54. Ibis: (1900-1907) Quarterly Journal of the British Ornithologists' Union, illustrated by Lodge
55. Jackson, C. E. (1975) *Bird Illustrators: Some Artists in Early Lithography*
56. Jackson, C. E. (1978) *Wood Engravings of Birds*
57. Jackson, Sir F. J. (1938) *The Birds of Kenya Colony and Uganda Protectorate*
58. Journal of the Bombay Natural History Society
59. Journal of the Federated Malay States Museums
60. Kelsall, J. E. and Munn, P. W. (1905) *The Birds of Hampshire and The Isle of Wight*
61. Kirkman, F. B. B. (1910-1913) *The British Bird Book*
62. Kirkman, F. B. B. and Hutchinson, H. G. ed. (1924 - new edn, 1936) *British Sporting Birds*
63. Kirkman, F. B. B. and Jourdain, F. C. R. (1930 - new edns) *British Birds*
64. Lascelles, Hon. G. W. (1971 - new edns) *The Art of Falconry 1892*, part of Cox and Lascelles
65. Lilford, Lord. (1885-1897) *Coloured Figures of the Birds of the British Islands*
66. Lilford, Lord. (1895) *Notes on the Birds of Northamptonshire and Neighbourhood*
67. Lodge, G. E. (1946) *Memoirs of an Artist Naturalist*
68. Lodge, R. B. (1906) *The Story of Hedgerow and Pond*
69. Mansel-Pleydell, J. C. (1888) *The Birds of Dorsetshire*
70. Mathews, G. M. (1910-1927) *The Birds of Australia*
71. Mavrogordato, J. G. (1960 - new edns) *A Hawk for the Bush*
72. Mavrogordato, J. G. (1966) *A Falcon in the Field*
73. Meinertzhagen, R. ed. (1930) *Nicoll's Birds of Egypt*
74. Meinertzhagen, R. (1954 - new edn, 1981) *Birds of Arabia*
75. Meinertzhagen, R. (1959) *Pirates and Predators*
76. Michell, E. B. (1900 - new edns) *The Art and Practice of Hawking*
77. Milliais, J. G. (1892) *Game Birds and Shooting Sketches*

78. Milliais, J. G. (1899) *A Breath from the Veldt*

79. Milliais, J. G. (1904-1906) *The Mammals of Great Britain and Ireland*

80. Milliais, J. G. (1913) *et al. British Deer and Ground Game, Dogs, Guns and Rifles - The Gun at Home and Abroad,* Vol. 2

81. Mitchell, F. S. (1892) *The Birds of Lancashire*

82. Nethersole-Thompson, D. (1975) *Pine Crossbills*

83. Neumann, A. H. (1898) *Elephant Hunting in East Equatorial Africa*

84. Ogilvie-Grant, W. R. (1912) *et al. British Game Birds and Wildfowl - The Gun at Home and Abroad,* Vol. 1

85. Parker, E. (1939 - new edns) *Predatory Birds of Great Britain*

86. Pitcher, E. and Velarde, R. (2009) *The Flying of Falcons*

87. Pycraft, W. P. (1910) *A History of Birds*

88. Rothschild, Hon L. W. (1907) *Extinct Birds*

89. Sands, T. (2012) *Wildlife in Trust: A Hundred Years of Nature Conservation*

90. Saunders, H. (1889 - new edns) *An Illustrated Manual of British Birds*

91. Savory, J. ed. (1986) *George Lodge, Artist Naturalist*

92. Schulze-Hagen, K. and Geus, A. ed. (2000) *Joseph Wolf (1820-1899): Tiermaler - Animal Painter*

93. Seebohm, H. (1883-1885) *A History of British Birds*

94. Seebohm, H. (1887) *The Geographical Distribution of the Family Charadriidae*

95. Selous, E. (1905) *Bird Life Glimpses*

96. Smith, R. B. (1905) *Bird Life and Bird Lore*

97. Stewart, H. E. (1897) *The Birds of our Country*

98. Swift, J. R. author/curator, (ed. by Mattox, W. G.) (2010) The Archives of Falconry, *Bibliotheca Accipitraria II, A Catalog of Books Ancient and Modern Relating to Falconry*

99. Thomas, W. B. and Collett, A. K. (1917) *Birds through the Year*

100. Thornton, T. A. (1896) *A Sporting Tour through the Northern Parts of England and Great Part of the Highlands of Scotland*

101. Upton, R. (1980) *A Bird in the Hand: Celebrated Falconers of the Past*

102. Upton, R. (1987) *O for a Falconer's Voice: Memories of the Old Hawking Club*

103. Vincent, J. and Lodge, G. E. (1911, 1980) *A Season of Birds: A Norfolk Diary*

104. Walsingham, Lord and Payne-Gallwey, Sir R. W. F. (1886 new edn, 1889) *Shooting: Moor and Marsh* (Badminton Library)

105. Walton, I. and Cotton, C. (ed. by Harting, J. E.) (1893) *The Complete Angler*

106. Watkins, W. (1903) *The Birds of Tennyson*

107. Webster, H. M. (ed. by Enderson, J. H.) (1988) *Game Hawking…at its very best - A Falconry Anthology*

108. Witherby, H. F. (1919) *A Practical Handbook of British Birds*

109. Witherby, H. F. Jourdain, F. C. R., Ticehurst, N. F. and Tucker, B. W. (1938-1941) *The Handbook of British Birds*

110. Wright, C. D. and Scott, J. (2004) *The Game Cook Book*

111. Yeates, G. K. (1948) *Bird Haunts in Northern Britain*

112. Zoological Society of London: (1900-1921) *Proceedings and Transactions,* Illustrated by Lodge

George Lodge also illustrated articles in magazines, these included; *The Badminton Magazine, The English Illustrated Magazine, The Field, The Illustrated London News* and *The Shooting Times & Country Magazine.* Lodge paintings were also used for Christmas cards by societies like the Camberley Natural History Society, the Association of Bird Watchers and Wardens, and the Royal Society for the Protection of Birds.

Freshwater Cliffs, Isle of Wight: Herring gulls mobbing a peregrine.
Oil on canvas.

# PICTURES EXHIBITED AT THE ROYAL ACADEMY BY GEORGE E. LODGE

1881 - Peregrines

1884 - Broken Slumbers

1886 - Roving Wild and Free

1888 - Peregrines

1889 - Master Stripes

1890 - Wild Duck

1891 - Brer Rabbit

1899 - We Two

1900 - Freshwater Cliffs, Isle of Wight: Herring gulls mobbing a peregrine

1905 - Ptarmigan Ground: Norway

1910 - Golden Eagle

1917 - In Arctic Norway

# Information about the George Edward Lodge Trust

## Aims of the Charity:
To advance education of the public in the artwork, life and skills of George Edward Lodge.

## Activities:
The website is devoted to portraying all aspects of the life of G.E. Lodge and will include:

- Biographical information
- Reproductions of his artwork
- Representations of his diaries and memorabilia belonging to him

The Trust will build up a directory of artwork and artefacts relating to G.E. Lodge, endeavouring to determine what is available, where it is located and whether it is possible to be viewed.

The Trust will make available artwork and artefacts for those wishing to gain a greater understanding of G.E. Lodge, his artwork and techniques.

The Trust will build up an historical picture of Falconry in the 19th and early 20th centuries based particularly upon the artwork, records and diaries of G.E. Lodge, but expanding to incorporate other sources as they become available.

## Trustees:

## Contact us:
The Trust welcomes support from anyone interested in the life and works of George Edward Lodge.

www.georgeedwardlodgetrust.co.uk
**Email:** info@georgeedwardlodgetrust.co.uk

*The Trust needs your support to succeed*

# GEORGE EDWARD LODGE

F.Z.S., F.R.E.S., Vice Pres. B.O.U.

## A biography

Written by Judith Magill

# GEORGE EDWARD LODGE

## A BIOGRAPHY

### I. INTRODUCTION

In the late 19th to mid 20th century, a brilliant man was working away, of whom the general public were virtually unaware. Only now it is becoming generally known that he was an artistic genius. So many ornithologists, artists, naturalists and children can still learn from him today.

He was relatively unknown due to his quiet modesty. He disliked being photographed and being placed at the centre of attention. He only exhibited his brilliant work when finances were low, then never the best of it, which he kept in his studio. He made his living from illustrating publications and selling commissioned pictures.

This man was George Edward Lodge, who was an artist, naturalist, ornithologist, taxidermist, lithographer, sculptor, writer and falconer. He illustrated over 100 publications and produced an immense number of pictures, so many he lost count after 1,000. Approximately 3,000 have been estimated in his life time.

*George Edward Lodge painting "Stratagem", a peregrine on a rook, 1894.*

# II. FAMILY

George Lodge was born at Horncastle, Lincolnshire, England, on 3rd December 1860. He was the fifth son and the seventh, of the twelve children of Rev. Samuel and Mary Brettingham Lodge.

The Rev. Samuel Lodge M.A., was born at Barking, Essex in 1829 and died at Scrivelsby in 1897. He was the youngest of 23 children of The Rev. Oliver Lodge, who had been married three times. Oliver's first wife, Dorcas Cromie, died without having children. His second wife, Anna Butler, gave birth to the first nine of the 23 children. His third wife, Anne Supple, mother of Samuel, gave birth to the remaining fourteen.

*Rev. Samuel Lodge, 1829-1897.*

Rev. Samuel Lodge was educated at Lincoln College, Oxford and took the B.A. degree in 1850 proceeding to M.A. in 1854. From 1851 to 1854 he was a classical master at Louth Grammar School. From 1854 to 1857 he was Curate of High Trynton, also from 1854 to 1870 he was Headmaster of Horncastle Grammar School and from 1876 to the time of his death, 1897, he was Canon of Lincoln Cathedral. In 1867, he became rector of the Parishes of Scrivelsby and Dalderby. The following year he was appointed Rural Dean of Horncastle. Scrivelsby Court was the home of the King's Champions. The Rev. Samuel had the Rectory built at Scrivelsby. The foundation stone was laid in 1869. Samuel had all the children press their hands in the wet concrete of the foundations. This they did except the eldest, Reginald, who had left home and was working in Marine Insurance for his uncle, Robert Lodge, Samuel's brother. The house was completed in 1870. George was nine years of age when they took up residence.

The Rev. Samuel researched the families of Marmion and Dymoke, the King's Champions. He wrote and published, *Scrivelsby, the Home of the Champions*. He dedicated it, "To Wife and Children and all who love a Happy Home."

George's mother, Mary Brettingham Lodge, was born in 1824 at Diss, Norfolk and died at Woodhall Spa in 1916. She was the seventh child of Thomas and Clara Maria Brettingham. Clara Maria was the daughter of Francis Wheatley R.A., famous for his paintings of the Cries of London. He was President of the Royal Academy and on his death in 1801, was followed by Joseph M.W. Turner. Francis Wheatley married Clara Maria Leigh, who was also an artist. These were George's great grandparents. Following the death of her husband Francis, Clara Maria Wheatley married Alexander Pope.

*Mary Brettingham Lodge, 1824-1916.*

Mary was an exquisite needle worker. She made the christening gowns for her babies and stitched tiny dolls out of the fingers of old kid gloves for her grandchildren. In her old age she occupied herself with her sewing, seldom leaving the house. The family would occasionally tell her "to change the thimble for a bonnet and go out" but she was very contented and had little desire to leave her home. Mary also made large, beautiful scrap books for her children. They had hand stitched linen pages, filled with lovely fine cut outs. Her grandchildren and great grandchildren also had the pleasure of gazing at these books, on special occasions.

George descended from a long line of large families, which was probably the reason for the closeness of his siblings, who all adored each other and their loving but strict parents. They were a very happy family. The children were encouraged to observe nature and wild life, each owning their own pet.

*Scrivelsby Rectory (rear view), circa 1890.*

Sadness struck the family in 1867 with the death of their three-day-old baby, Eleanor Constance and again in 1886 when Herbert Barton died at the age of 31 years, in Calcutta. It was a devastating blow in 1890 when 35-year-old Walter Macnamara died at Scrivelsby, of suspected appendicitis.

The eldest in the family, Reginald Badham, at the age of 16 years had left home before they moved to Scrivelsby. He was an artist, naturalist, author and pioneer of bird photography, awarded Medallist Royal Photographic Society. He spent many hours, with George's help, pushing his camera in a wheelbarrow over the Lincolnshire Fens during his frequent visits to the Rectory. He was a

*Reginald Badham Lodge with his camera in Woodhall Woods.*

very gentle man. When their father died it was Reg who the family turned to, to comfort their mother with his gentle ways.

The family had a very faithful friend in Job Raithby, who lived with his wife Mary in a Glebe cottage near the Rectory. He had a crippled son, Moses Henry and three daughters. He was a tenant farmer who worked the nearby fields and did extra domestic work at the Rectory, cared for the gardens and also drove the wagonette for the family. They always spoke highly of Raithby and he was very much part of their life.

These were very happy years for George.

*Raithby in the Wagonette at the Rectory entrance.*

## III. Childhood

George Lodge first showed interest in birds when he was a very small boy. Someone told him he could catch a sparrow if you put salt on its tail. After this, he always carried salt in his pocket!

George and his two younger brothers, Alexander John and Arthur Brettingham, were the closest of friends and were frequently up to harmless mischief, having to be reprimanded by their father. One instance was when the ice broke while skating, instead of attending Sunday Church. Unfortunately, they had to walk home past the Church, very wet, just as the congregation was leaving… it was very bad timing! Only once, they threw walnuts from the large walnut tree in the garden at the visiting grocer and his horse. After another sedate visit to Father's office, they were made to pick a large bag of walnuts, take them to the grocer and apologise. On another occasion they decided to visit the old Scrivelsby Court. It had been vacant for some years as the owners were not in residence. At the sight of the armour in the great hall, temptation was too much, it had to be tried. Alick was used as the model. When guilt overcame them, they took it off and put it carefully back but the helmet with visor was firmly stuck. It was a very worrying time as the thought of having to confront Father in this state was not good. It took some time to free Alick and they never visited the Court again. Another instance was when they were playing near a mill pond, one fell in. Someone rushed in to tell the miller to turn off the wheel. The miller was heard to utter "it's probably one of those dreadful Lodge boys, well, there are plenty more."

The children roamed far and wide in the area, spending long hours in the derelict Tattershalls Castle, which George later painted for his younger sister,

*Lion Gate entrance of Scrivelsby Court, "The hole" can be seen at lower right.*

Mary Beatrice, who they affectionately called Sissy. They studied and watched wild life, birds in particular by George. They went bird nesting, building up a collection of eggs, but only ever taking one from the nests.

When they were small children, Alice Spilman, their nurse, took them on walks in the area near the Rectory. Whenever they passed the Lion Gate, at the entrance to Scrivelsby Court, behind Nurse's back they retrieved their hidden nail and picked a small hole in the stonework of the Gate. The hole grew larger each time and can be plainly seen in old photographs of the famous Lion Gate, which has long since been repaired.

George was a small boy when he was taken on a 300 acre cover shoot. The keeper kindly lent him his gun and he shot a woodcock. The only one shot on the day. It was given to him, so he stuffed it very badly but replaced it at a later date with a better one. He was 12 years old when he stuffed an owl. This was the beginning of his wonderful taxidermy.

Their mother encouraged reading and often read to the children. As they grew older she read The Venerable Adam Bede to them. With their wicked sense of humour, they would all sit up and wait for what they called "A Dam Beady."

Their mother also had the girls learn to cook and keep house, envisaging the future when there would be no help.

At Christmas time they built snowmen in the garden and hung holly from a hook in the nursery ceiling. They had a very happy childhood.

*George and Mary Beatrice Lodge, circa 1865.*

# IV. Schooling

George went to school at the Horncastle Grammar School. This old school was founded in 1652 by Edward, Lord Clintan and Saye, The Lord High Admiral of England. It was "The Free Grammar School of Queen Elizabeth I" to educate boys. George showed promise in drawing and painting, so in 1847 at the age of 14 years he was sent to the Lincoln School of Art, where he won several prizes. George Adrian was a taxidermist there, from whom the young George would learn.

At the age of 16, George went to learn wood engraving at Whymper's London Wood engravers, in which he excelled. He illustrated publications including *The Illustrated London News*.

GRAMMAR SCHOOL.

*Horncastle Grammar School.*

Photography eventually lessened the sale of George's wood cuts. In 1900, on a visit to Norway, he wrote to Arthur saying, "I am still subsisting on borrowed money but am hoping for times to improve as I have gone in for lithography on stone, I am in hopes of doing a good deal of this sort of work in the way of birds for the museum. I have already done some for them and they have promised me more, as they are very dissatisfied with [the artist], who mostly has done their work, and have as good as promised me all the work they would otherwise put in his hands. I have also lately done a little work for the *Badminton Magazine*, and hope to do more, as I have accepted their prices, which are very low, and they are pleased with my work (so they ought to be considering that they get best work for bad prices). I have also been doing some work for the Bombay Nat. Hist. Society, and they have promised me more. In the mean time I am staying here with a friend who has a good salmon river, so I paint all day and

I think I shall be able to sell most of the things I am doing here, as the valley is full of English people, fishing salmon, and therefore plenty of money. I have already sold some of them, so hope to get back to England with a bit of money in my pocket after paying all expenses. So I think that things are decidedly beginning to pick up." These were very hard years for George, his mother and Arthur helped with his finances until he could repay them.

George studied under Joseph Wolf, who he regarded as the greatest draftsman of birds of all time.

*Joseph Wolf.*

## V. London

For 39 years, from 1881 to 1920, George lived in London. He studied and sketched animals at London Zoo and regularly visited museums. He collected twigs and foliage from parks to use as backgrounds for his paintings of small birds. He requested the family in the country, to send that which he called "rubbish", to use for the same purpose. They co-operated. He always drew and painted from nature.

George liked tempera to illustrate books. This was his favourite medium as being made with egg yolk, it dried quickly. He was a fast worker and tempera could be painted over and did not run, unlike gouache, which is made from gum arabic and is slow drying. During the war when eggs were hard to obtain, George worked more in watercolours, oils and sometimes gouache.

For 30 years George's studios at various stages were in Collingham Place, Verulium Buildings Grays Inn, Thurloe Square and Holborn Viaduct. Pictures from these addresses were exhibited at the Royal Academy. His brothers Alick and Arthur sometimes resided with him.

George became a keen falconer and was well known in the streets because he carried a hawk on his fist. He said "If a hawk was calm in the noise of the city, it would work well in the country".

He spent many happy visits to the estate of his falconer friend, Thomas J. Mann, to whom he was introduced to by Edward Blair Michell. Michell at one time was a legal advisor to the King of Siam and was writing a book on falconry, which he asked George to illustrate. Michell suggested that he go to Thomas Mann to observe falconry, which George did, introducing him to the sport and leading to his lifelong friendship with Thomas Mann. He also went hawking on Salisbury Plain and other parts of Wiltshire with his hawking companions, including Jack Mavrogordato, Capt. Gilbert Blaine and Dr. H.O. Blandford. Jack Mavrogordato asked him to design a hawk with outstretched wings for a weathervane, which can still be seen at Tilshead.

George was an active member of the Old Hawking Club.

He travelled far and wide, studying and painting birds and animals. Raptors were his greatest love and he produced his best work painting them. He went to Sweden, Norway, Ceylon, Japan and the West Indies. He also stayed on Garden Island, north of Long Island in the U.S.A. He loved the Shetland Islands and Scottish Highlands where he went stalking and shooting. Wherever he went he carried pocket sketch books, filled them with miniature sketches of birds, animals and suitable backgrounds for his subjects. George was in the habit of positioning himself in very precarious places to sketch backgrounds. He painted several pictures of Peregrines flying off the chalk cliffs of the Sussex coast and another was Horn Head, Donegal coast, Ireland. George painted the magnificent painting of Red Banks, on the coast of North Roe Island, Shetland (42 x 60 inches).

He worked on these cliffs while waiting to sight the Albino Sea Eagle which had lived and nested there for thirty years. He suffered extreme cold while sketching it and waited some time for the eagle to appear. Then one day the eagle flew from behind the cliffs being mobbed by hooded crows, enabling him to add it to the picture. The family were worried George would come to grief while working in these dangerous places.

The family were used to receiving strange requests from George. On one occasion, Mary was left to rear a caterpillar while he was in Norway. They were always happy to oblige.

He wanted to paint the Australian birds, especially the colours of the parrots but he suffered very debilitating sea sickness, often being carried off the ship at his destination. This prevented him from undertaking the long voyage to Australia, where he had two brothers, who he dearly wished to visit. One was his older brother Francis Wheatley Lodge, who was Commissioner of Police in Western Australia and the other, Arthur Brettingham Lodge, who farmed in the district of York, 100km east of Perth. Both were married with families.

*Left to right, Alexander John Lodge (Alick), Arthur Brettingham Lodge and George, circa 1883.*

# VI. The War Years

In 1916, during the Great War, George posed as an artist for three to four months on the north coast of Norway. He was sent by the Admiralty and was to send back paintings of eider ducks' nests. It was believed this could have meant he had seen homes or harbours of enemy submarines. It would have been a very worrying time for the family had they known.

George's mother died in 1916. After Rev. Samuel died in 1897, she had to move from the Rectory to live in a house called Sunnyside in Tattershalls Rd., Woodhall Spa. Her youngest daughters, Mary and Edith, went with her. Edith then married The Rev. Henry Benwell M.A., Vicar of Woodhall Spa, so Mary, who was a trained nurse, cared for her mother. The family were devastated when they had to leave the Rectory and never returned to see it. They only ever went to the church to care for the family graves. It was many years before George and Alick went back to visit their old haunts. They stayed at The Bull in Horncastle feeling rather depressed.

In 1920, George moved from London to Camberley, Surrey and took his sister Mary with him.

The day World War II was declared, George and his hawking companions took their merlins to a hill near Tilshead and after giving them a chunk of beef, wished them luck then released them onto Salisbury Plain.

During World War II he was active in the Army Volunteer Reserve and in his spare time, knitted scarves for the Army and Air Force. At one stage he had completed 330, one yard long (approximately 90cm). He then wanted navy blue wool, to make them for the Navy.

In 1942, George's older widowed sister Clara, who had married her cousin Francis Heawood Lodge, died. She was being cared for by her unmarried daughter, Brenda. As Mary was ageing and having difficulty caring for George, Brenda moved to Camberley and took her mother's help, Maud James with her, to care for both George and Mary.

Mary blessed the coming of Brenda as it had saved her from a breakdown. She was tired and suffered from arthritis, the house was cold and she was aged 81 years and George 82. Mary died in 1947.

They were very hard years with food in short supply and no one wanted to buy paintings.

George missed his friends and wrote to his brother Arthur saying, "Young Officers in Cavalry Regiments that I have known well, chiefly keen hawking men, have been killed." He wrote of Scrivelsby days and wished they still lived there.

George's brother, Frank, had died in Western Australia. Arthur was still living in the country district of York. His son, Colin Lodge, was managing their farm, "Marley". They corresponded regularly with George and the family. Arthur's daughter Lorna Lodge (later Mrs Lorna Barrett-Lennard), along with Colin's wife Muriel and Frank's widow, Marian, organised regular food parcels to be sent to the family in England throughout the war, until the mid 1950s. One day a happy letter of thanks arrived from George to his niece Lorna, saying how he and Brenda had been able to entertain some young Army friends billeted near Camberley, who liked to visit and see the paintings. He wrote, "We had four young soldier friends who dropped in to see us and the pictures, when they were in the neighbourhood. As a parcel of food had arrived we had a picnic tea in the studio, sitting on little stools around little tables and dipped into the parcel. The happiest afternoon we have ever spent."

*Hawkhouse, circa 1948.*

*Left to right, Clara Lodge, Phyllis Lodge, Brenda Lodge at Boscombe, 1913.*

*Mary Beatrice Lodge (Sissy).*

*Maud James.*

*Brenda Lodge.*

When George moved to Upper Park Road, Camberley in 1920 he called his house Hawkhouse and built a studio onto it. It was an enormous studio (in later years, new owners built two bedrooms and two bathrooms above it). The walls were packed with his beautiful paintings, large and small. The largest was 6 x 5ft. (180 x 150cm). He kept all his best work and he photographed any he sold privately.

The studio was filled with cases of brilliant taxidermy. Beside his own work, he hunted for specimens in antique shops and bought anything worthwhile. He relaxed the specimen and remounted it. There were cabinets of eggs and drawer upon drawer filled with an enormous number of unframed watercolours. George painted in tempera, watercolours and oils. His favourite medium remained tempera, often using it with watercolour. He was a quick painter but liked to spend at least two weeks on a work putting his heart, mind and soul into it. He became so involved in it that before commencing a new work, he would have to spend one or two days changing his mind set from the bird he had been working on, to the next to be painted. He excelled in painting the character and nature of birds he portrayed. Falconers could recognise their own bird, if it was painted in a group of the same species.

*Taxidermy of two peregrine falcons, Celia and Farthingale.*

George did all his framing, wood cuts, etc. in his studio. In 1947, when he realised he could no longer go stalking and shooting, he set to and copied all the records of his experiences and research, producing a large amount of written work. He recorded all his findings from the hands-on research undertaken throughout his life. His falconry diary contained 241 pages, including eight pages on how a peregrine strikes its quarry with its feet. His research and notes, containing hundreds of pages, hold a wealth of knowledge for falconers, ornithologists and naturalists.

He also wrote and published his memoirs, *Memoirs of an Artist Naturalist*. Unfortunately this was at the end of World War II when paper and plates were of very poor quality, affecting the reproductions of the illustrations and general appearance of the book.

Birds were George's life and he illustrated many science books. When doing this, he liked to paint the birds in their natural habitats, which were always done from nature. The rocks, trees, branches, grasses, foliage and flowers that formed the backgrounds were all scientifically correct. He said this was part of the nature of the bird. The books contained many beautiful pictures, rather than single, isolated specimens. He never used a camera as he felt it took the life out of the subject.

Archibald Thorburn, George's contemporary and friend, was asked by the New Zealand Government to paint all the birds of that country. He declined, suggesting they contact George Lodge, which they did. George undertook the commission. As he was unable to travel to New Zealand, he used skins from the collections of Gregory M Matthews and the British Museum. He was never keen to paint in this manner but being the only possible way, he proceeded, producing magnificent pictures but he was unable to include all the natural habitats to these birds. The editorial was written by Sir Charles Fleming. Unfortunately the book was published after George's death, so sadly he never saw the end result.

George's life ambition was to paint all the British birds in one publication. He achieved this when he was asked by Dr. David Bannerman to illustrate a set of twelve volume books, *The Birds of the British Isles*, which he wished to publish. George produced 384 full sized coloured plates by August 1947. He was then 87 years of age. His right eye was giving trouble as it developed double vision. Bannerman then asked if he could paint five more pictures. George did this by blacking out the right side of his glasses. It was a worry that by using one eye, the standard of his work would be lowered but there was no change. The pictures were perfection. Sadly, George lived to see only the first two volumes published but his ambition was achieved. George's desire, along with Bannerman's full agreement, was to dedicate this work to Queen Elizabeth II. To Bannerman's disappointment, at the completion of publication this was overlooked but a set was gifted to the Queen, who was delighted and requested it be housed at Balmoral. Queen Elizabeth, the Queen Mother, also received a set.

George formed the George Lodge Trust in 1944, at the suggestion of Robert Grant of Oliver and Boyd, to help pay for the printing of the Bannerman books. George contributed £5,000 towards this.

*George aged 90 years.*

George seldom dated his pictures, until he reached the age of 90 years, after which he did. The reason being, some people visiting the studio thought that pictures decreased in value with age. On one occasion, someone bought a painting and told him they had bought one many years previously, "what should we do with that"? He told them "throw it out"! He always undervalued his work to people. His niece Lorna, in Western Australia, asked if she could buy a painting for her new sitting room. George's response was "I do not know why you want to spoil your nice new room with my old rubbish." He then sent her a beautiful watercolour and tempera painting, of a peregrine falcon, flying off the chalk cliffs of the Sussex coast and insisted it was a gift for her birthday. He signed and dated it, 1951.

The studio was very cold in the winter and as he aged, he found it difficult to work there. He had a small gas heater, which was most inadequate for the size of the room and the skylight shed very poor light and warmth on dull days.

George enjoyed the company of young people and welcomed anyone who wished to call and see his pictures. Artists were always encouraged and he was very ready to give help when asked.

Field Marshal Lord Alanbrooke called several times. He liked to just sit, look at the pictures on the walls and watch George paint. He found the studio a haven of peace, where he could relax.

*The hawk weathervane designed by George.*

*George in his studio (Lorna Barrett-Lennard's picture top left), 1951.*

## VIII. A Summary

George Lodge never married. In his younger days there was someone special but the family were not happy about it. Letters to his Australian relatives, now and again, showed a slight hint of sadness that he had no immediate family of his own.

It was a very traumatic time for the family when the Rev. Samuel died at Scrivelsby in 1897. Apart from the two brothers in Western Australia, all the family gathered at their old home for his last few days. They knew the rectory had to be left for the following rector and their mother would have to live elsewhere. It was very hard for her as she had not left the district for years and the family were concerned as to how she would cope. In a very sad letter written at the time by George to Arthur, he added "Mann died of consumption last week. I am afraid it is an awful blow to his family he was only 49. I wasn't able to go to his funeral as of course at this time I cannot leave here." He then described how all the family were and "Alick shoots rabbits in the field with my rifle and we devour them." His father died the following day.

Hawkhouse was a very happy household. Brenda was a great animal lover and she always had numerous cats and rabbits. Cats were not ideal where garden birds were encouraged. She wrote to the family saying "I can no longer live without a cat, so have one hidden. Uncle George does not know!" In a letter received later from George, he said "she has a cat and thinks I do not know." He was having a lot of fun watching Brenda keep a hidden cat.

Brenda was kind and amiable and made tea for the numerous people who visited George in his studio, Field Marshal Lord Alanbrooke among them. In 1947, Lord Alanbrooke had commissioned George to paint 24 Birds of Prey and six Owls. George was then 87 years of age and painting with his right eye covered, but the commission was completed.

In 1947, George gave up doing small work because he could only use one eye but was able to cope with an abundance of commissions for larger pictures. He wrote to Lorna saying he was "deaf, blind and stupid but still blundering about with his painting."

In August 1948, George wrote to the family, "I have plenty of work in hand. At present am doing 16 drawings in colour for a small book on Mountain Birds (British) and have a few larger pictures to do so I am kept out of mischief. In the olden days at this time of the year I should have been in Scotland shooting grouse but I shall never see a live grouse again. Grouse are the most beautiful and most sporting of all the British Game Birds. When my time comes, I should like to be buried on a Scottish hillside, all amongst the heather and the grouse and the stags and the eagles. Incidentally, I should like very much to have a day's shooting in our House of Commons, I bet I would shoot jolly straight!" The writer of the small book on Mountain Birds was George's friend, Robert Coombes.

On the 31st December 1949, he wrote again to the family saying, "I am still able to do my painting work and have several commissions and my agents in London want another exhibition of my things for next Christmas. My doing them is a bit slow now, owing to having only one available eye and getting a bit fumble fisted owing to old age."

Brenda wrote on the 10th of June 1953, "Uncle George V well and drawing a hawk with outstretched wings, for some of his friends who want a weather cock. He sits out in the garden on fine afternoons."

He was lean and very straight. His handwriting was as clear and steady as 20 years previously. Breathlessness prevented him from exercise but he never lost his sense of humour or interest in the world around him. He enjoyed his pipe and a glass of ale.

*Edith Lodge in her electric wheelchair, aged 84 years, 1948.*

Edith, his widowed sister, lived eight miles away at Fleet. She was a caring person and often helped their older sister Nora and for a time lived with her. Nora was losing her sight and had had a sad life. She married Ernest Myers and four of their five children died in her life time. Edith was very active in her youth and had once bicycled 30 miles with her friends, Hugh Mann and his wife. In her old age she bought an electric wheelchair. George wrote in 1948, "Aunt Edith came for afternoon tea for my birthday. She has got some sort of electric wheelbarrow on which she goes scooting about. As she is 84 it is rather risky but that's her lookout."

As previously written, George loved young people and enjoyed the visits of John Southern (later O.B.E.) who was aged 19 years and George 90. Not liking

*Nora Lodge who the siblings called
"The beauty of the family".*

to be called Mr. Lodge, he insisted John call him Uncle George. The Mann family, some of George's oldest friends, affectionately called him Uncle Dick, because they said he was always drawing "dickie birds".

George's work was wide and varied. He designed four silver mustard pots in the shape of Dutch Hoods, replicas of falcon hoods. The spoons had the shape of lure wings on the end of the handles. These were for his close falconry friends. He also designed tiny tie pins in the shape of falcon hoods and he designed the logo for the British Falconers Club.

He drew the red kite, for the logo of the Royal Society of Wild Life Trust and in 1945 he drew a kookaburra for the Royal Australian Air Force badge. He also designed two badges for the Royal Air Force.

*Mustard pot and spoon designed by George.*

In 1900, he did work for the Bombay Natural History Society.

During his life George belonged to many natural history societies, including The Camberley Natural History Society and he was a member of the Norfolk Naturalist Trust. He was also on the Committee of the British section of the International Society for the Preservation of Wild Fowl. He was a member of the British Ornithologists' Union, elected in 1945, and was the only Artist Naturalist to be so honoured. He was a Fellow of the Zoological Society of London and he bequeathed a large amount of work to the Natural History Museum.

George was ahead of his time in the encouragement of setting aside nature reserves. He was one of a group who established the first nature reserve in Britain, for the benefit of future generations.

He did all these things, along with all the publications he illustrated, his writing and diaries, numerous sketch books filled with exquisite miniature paintings, drawings and written accounts of his findings. Lastly, he left his taxidermy and the thousands of beautiful pictures, for the world to learn from and enjoy. He worked until only a matter of weeks before his death.

*Brenda and George on his 93rd Birthday, 1953.*

## IX. The End

George and his family frequently corresponded. Their numerous letters to Arthur, the youngest in the family living in Western Australia, were all kept, making valuable references to which this account of George's life has mainly been based, along with the family stories which were told by Arthur.

George lived life to the full. In his London days, he never missed a Gilbert and Sullivan opera, enjoying in particular the humour, harmony and rhythmic music. He sent the scores of all the operas to Lorna, who he knew played the piano for her family.

He was very fit and blessed with good health. It was only latterly, in his late 80s, that he developed a rare and painful condition, affecting a nerve in his jaw. This in turn, affected the sight in his right eye, causing double vision, but it was only for a few months he was unable to paint. After some time in St. Thomas's Hospital, London, he was able to return to his painting but with the use of his left eye only.

In his last years, he lived quietly at Hawkhouse with Brenda and dear, faithful Maud. On warm sunny days he sat in his deck chair in the garden, wrapped in his old green hawking jacket with the brass buttons, tweed cap and an empty pipe in his mouth. He always had a handful of meal worms and crumbs, for the little birds who befriended him. These were a robin, chaffinches, sparrows and blue tits, which would be around his feet and on his knees.

*George in his deck chair feeding the birds at Hawkhouse.*

On the 5th February 1954, George died in his 94th year.

He was a kind, quiet, modest English gentleman who was very dearly loved, respected and sadly missed by all who knew him. He was an artistic genius.

His service at the Garden of Remembrance, Brookwood, was attended by many. His ashes were returned and interred beside his dear parents and with his brother Walter, his sister Mary and baby sister Eleanor, at their beloved St. Benedicts Church, Scrivelsby, Lincolnshire.

Maxwell Knight, naturalist and broadcaster, wrote the obituary of George Edward Lodge, for the Camberley News. In it he stated, "For well over half a century he could justly be acclaimed as one of the world's leading bird artists and at the peak of his power, there was no one equal to him on the depicting of game birds and birds of prey."

Thank you Uncle George, for the enrichment you gave and will continue to give to so many, through your wonderful work and memories.

Judith Magill, his great niece.

Some Observations on bird painting.

This is not an easy subject to write about, and
must not be approached in anything like assurance
or dogmatism; as every one who ~~goes in for this~~
studies ~~branch of~~ art has his own ideas and methods,
and, quite rightly, follows and uses them in order
to obtain the results that appeal to him.
Results will be got by different ~~people~~ by entirely
different methods; and who shall say that this
or that is the ~~t~~ correct way of preceedure?
Individualism is necessary in all branches of art,
if only to eliminate the wearysomeness of monotony.
It is to be supposed that modern artists would
say that ~~painting~~ birds is not art at all, but only
"copying from Nature". But those who have given
their lives to painting pictures of birds will say
that few things in Nature are more beautiful and
full of grace than are birds; and therefore, why
not "copy" them? Especially so when one has the
sense to realize how extremely difficult it is to
"copy" a living bird.
You cannot requisition a living bird and direct it
to sit to you in a certain pose for a certain time as
you can a human model. You are entirely dependant
upon whatever attitude the bird happens momentarily
to place itself, and you may wait a lifetime without
even/